Thriving as an ADHD Mom

Proven Systems to Organize Life, Balance Work & Family

Patty R. Adams

Table of Contents

Introduction 1

Chapter 1: The Perfectly Imperfect ADHD Mom: Embracing Your Neurodivergent
Motherhood Journey 5

    Understanding Your ADHD Brain: The Neuroscience of Maternal Thinking 7

    From Chaos to Creativity: Reframing ADHD Traits as Superpowers 9

    Building Your Support System: Creating a Network That Gets You 12

Chapter 2: Kitchen Table Command Center: Simple Systems for Household Chaos
Control 17

    The Visual Command Center: Setting Up Your Kitchen Table Hub 18

    Paper Taming Techniques: From Chaos to Clarity 20

    Time Blocking and Family Routines: Making the System Stick 23

Chapter 3: Mind Like a Browser with 100 Tabs Open: Managing the Mental Load of
Motherhood 28

    Digital Brain Dumping: Using Technology to Capture the Mental Load 29

    Task Triage: Prioritizing When Everything Feels Urgent 31

    Creating Mental Bandwidth: Strategies for Clearing Mental Clutter 33

Chapter 4: From Scattered to Structured: Creating Routines That Actually Stick
(No, Really!) 38

    Building Flexible Routines: The ADHD-Friendly Framework 39

    Transition Mastery: Smoothing the Rough Edges of Daily Life 42

    The Power of Habit Stacking: Creating Sustainable Change 44

Chapter 5: Working Mom Wizardry: Juggling Career and Kids with an ADHD Brain
.... 50

    Task Switching Mastery: Transitioning Between Work and Home Modes 51

    The ADHD-Friendly Office: Creating a Workspace That Works for You 53

    Calendar Choreography: Syncing Family and Professional Commitments 56

Chapter 6: The Digital Mom's Toolbox: Tech Solutions for the ADHD Parent's Brain
.... 62

    Digital Organization: Choosing and Using the Right Apps for Your ADHD Brain 63

    Smart Home Solutions: Automating Routines and Reminders 65

    Digital Boundaries: Managing Tech Without Getting Overwhelmed 67

Chapter 7: When Mom's Brain Goes Zoom: Using Hyperfocus and Creativity as
Superpowers 72

    Harnessing Hyperfocus: Channeling Intense Attention for Maximum Impact 73

    The Creative ADHD Brain: Problem-Solving Outside the Box 75

    Building Bridges Between Hyperfocus and Daily Life: Creating Sustainable Systems 78

Chapter 8: The 'Me Time' Mission: Self-Care Strategies for the Overwhelmed ADHD Mom **84**

Micro-Moments of Self-Care: Finding Peace in Five-Minute Intervals.............................85

Energy Management vs. Time Management: Understanding Your Personal Battery.........87

Building Boundaries: Learning to Say No Without Guilt.. 90

Chapter 9: Family Team Building: Teaching Kids to Thrive with Your ADHD Leadership.. **96**

Creating a Neurodiversity-Affirming Home Environment: Celebrating Different Thinking Styles...97

Family Systems That Stick: Collaborative Problem-Solving Techniques 99

Building Resilience Together: Teaching Kids to Navigate Challenges with Confidence ...102

Chapter 10: Building Your Village: Creating Support Systems That Understand ADHD Motherhood **108**

Finding Your Tribe: Connecting with Other ADHD Parents...109

Communication Strategies: Explaining ADHD Needs to Family and Friends 112

Building Reciprocal Support Systems: Give and Take in ADHD Relationships............... 114

Conclusion..**120**

Bibliography **124**

Thank You for Reading!

I hope you found *Thriving as an ADHD Mom: Proven Systems to Organize Life, Balance Work & Family* helpful and enjoyable!
Your feedback is invaluable to me and helps others discover this book.

If you could take a moment to **leave a review**, I'd greatly appreciate it. Scan the QR code below to leave your review:

Visit the Cantelune Press website for more compassionate books that meet you where you are!

https://cantelunepress.com/

Thank you,

Patty R. Adams

Introduction

I found my son's homework in the freezer again. Not just tucked away in a corner, mind you, but perfectly centered between a bag of frozen peas and last week's grocery list, with a light dusting of frost creating tiny ice crystals along the edges of his math worksheet. For a moment, I stood there, freezer door wide open, cold air swirling around my feet, and let out a laugh that started somewhere deep in my belly. This wasn't a mistake; it was a perfect snapshot of my ADHD mom life, complete with the ironic twist that at least I'd found the homework before it became completely frozen solid.

I snapped a quick photo to share with my ADHD moms' support group (we have a dedicated channel just for our creative "filing system" discoveries), added "set up a homework command center" to my ever-growing list of ingenious solutions to try, and silently celebrated that I'd evolved from the days when such discoveries would have left me in tears.

Welcome to the wonderfully complex world of ADHD motherhood, where conventional parenting advice often falls spectacularly flat, and success looks wildly different from those perfectly curated Instagram feeds. If you've ever found yourself wondering how other moms seem to effortlessly juggle work meetings, school schedules, and household management while you're struggling to remember if you packed your kids' lunches (or even ate lunch yourself), I want you to know something important: you're not failing; you're navigating life with a beautifully unique brain in a world designed for neurotypical thinking.

I've learned through my own journey that this book isn't about fixing what isn't broken or transforming you into someone else's version of a perfect mother. Instead, it's about understanding and embracing your wonderfully wired brain while developing practical strategies that actually work for the way you think and process information. Together, we'll explore how to create systems that stick, harness your ADHD superpowers (yes, they're real!), and build a support network that understands and celebrates your neurodivergent journey.

Through these pages, you'll discover that those traits you've been fighting against, your ability to hyperfocus, think outside the box, or notice details others miss, can become your greatest parenting strengths. We'll dive into real-world solutions for managing the mental load of motherhood, establishing routines that bend without breaking, and maintaining your career without losing your sanity.

What you won't find here are rigid rules or one-size-fits-all solutions. Instead, I'm offering you battle-tested strategies from other ADHD moms, adaptable systems that work with your natural tendencies rather than against them, and permission to create your own unique path to parenting success. Think of this book as a heart-to-heart conversation with a friend who truly gets it; someone who understands why you might need to set three different alarms for school pickup or why you're most productive doing laundry at midnight.

Throughout these chapters, you'll meet other mothers who've walked this path and transformed their daily struggles into stepping stones, their perceived weaknesses into unexpected strengths, and their chaos into controlled creativity. Their stories will remind you that you're part of a larger community of amazing women who are redefining what successful motherhood looks like through an ADHD lens.

Remember, your ADHD isn't a barrier to being an incredible mother; it's part of what makes you uniquely equipped to raise children who understand resilience, creativity, and the beauty of thinking differently. Whether you're newly diagnosed, long-time diagnosed, or still exploring your neurodivergent journey, you'll find tools and insights to help you thrive, not just survive, in your role as a mother.

So grab your favorite beverage (even if you've already reheated it four times), find your comfy spot (or embrace the beautiful chaos around you), and prepare to discover how your ADHD traits can become your parenting superpowers. We're about to embark on a transformative journey together, one where we'll turn your unique way of experiencing the world into your greatest strength as a mother.

You've got this, and I'm right here with you, every wonderfully scattered step of the way.

Chapter 1:

The Perfectly Imperfect ADHD Mom: Embracing Your Neurodivergent Motherhood Journey

Like many women, I came to understand my ADHD journey later in life, often after years of feeling like I was somehow failing at motherhood despite my best efforts. The path to embracing our neurodivergent minds isn't always straightforward, but it can lead to profound transformations in how we approach parenting, work, and life itself.

In this chapter, we'll dive deep into what it truly means to navigate motherhood with an ADHD brain. Beyond the daily struggles of lost permission slips and forgotten appointments, we'll discover how our unique way of thinking can actually become our greatest parenting asset.

Take Jennifer's story; I'll never forget how she described that pivotal moment in the grocery store parking lot. Tears streaming down her face, she sat clutching her third shopping list of the week. The previous two had vanished into what she called the "black hole of mom's purse," along with her favorite pen and that birthday party invitation she was supposed to RSVP to last week. The harsh fluorescent lights of the parking lot illuminated her dashboard, where her phone buzzed relentlessly with texts about the PTA meeting she'd missed. The familiar wave of shame washed over her, that crushing feeling of letting everyone down yet again.

But then something shifted. Jennifer remembered her ADHD coach's words: "Different isn't a deficit." Taking a deep breath, she reached for her phone and opened her voice notes app. Instead of writing another list that would inevitably disappear, she recorded everything she needed, her voice slightly shaky but growing stronger with each item. As she walked into the store, earbuds in place and shopping list playing in her own voice, she felt something new; not shame, but pride. She wasn't doing things the "normal" way, but she was doing them her way, and for the first time in weeks, she'd complete her grocery shopping without forgetting half the items she needed.

This transformation, from fighting against our ADHD traits to working with them, is at the heart of what we'll explore together. We'll discover how to turn our tendency for creative problem-solving, our spontaneity, and even our moments of hyperfocus into powerful tools that can enhance our parenting rather than hinder it.

Throughout this chapter, we'll examine practical strategies for shifting our perspective from "fixing" our ADHD to embracing it as part of who we are. I'll share real-world techniques for working with our unique brain wiring, methods for building on our natural strengths, and systems that actually work for us rather than against us.

Remember, there's no one-size-fits-all approach to being an ADHD mom. What works beautifully for one of us might be a complete disaster for another, and that's perfectly okay. Our goal isn't to force ourselves into some idealized version of motherhood, but to discover and embrace our own unique path, one that honors both our challenges and our gifts. Together, we'll learn how to transform our perceived weaknesses into unexpected strengths, creating a parenting style that's authentically our own.

Understanding Your ADHD Brain: The Neuroscience of Maternal Thinking

Sarah's hands trembled as she stared at the jumble of papers scattered across her kitchen counter. School permission slips mingled with grocery lists, while sticky notes in various stages of curl clung desperately to the edges of her laptop. The morning sun streaming through the window illuminated the chaos in stark detail, making her heart race faster. She'd been up since 4 AM, determined to finally get organized, but instead found herself deep in a rabbit hole of research about different organizational systems, none of which seemed to fit the way her brain worked.

I know this scene intimately because I've lived it countless times. Like many ADHD moms, I've spent years trying to force my beautifully complex brain into systems designed for neurotypical minds.[1] The result? Frustration, shame, and a constant feeling of falling short.

Let's talk about what's really happening in our ADHD brains. Science shows us that our prefrontal cortex, that vital command center for planning and organization, processes information differently.[3] When you find yourself forgetting important appointments despite three reminder apps, or hyperfocusing on organizing the pantry at midnight while tomorrow's lunch boxes sit empty, that's your unique neural wiring at work.[3]

Take Michelle's story. She reached out to me after a particularly challenging morning, where she'd discovered her daughter's science project materials in the trunk of her car, two days after the project was due. "I'd remembered buying everything," she told me, tears in her voice. "But somehow, the supplies never made it from the car to the house. My brain registered 'buy project materials' as 'complete project' and moved on to the next urgent thing." This isn't a failure of motherhood; it's a perfect example of how ADHD affects our executive functioning.[3]

Our maternal brains are constantly processing an overwhelming amount of information. For those of us with ADHD, this process looks more like a pinball machine than a filing system.[4] Ideas, thoughts, and responsibilities bounce around with incredible energy and speed. While this can make traditional organizing challenging, it also gives us unique strengths.

When your child comes to you with an unexpected problem, your brain's ability to make rapid, creative connections often leads to innovative solutions. That same 'distraction' that makes it hard to focus during PTA meetings might help you notice subtle changes in your child's mood that others miss. Your tendency to hyperfocus, while challenging when it pulls you into reorganizing the garage at midnight, can become a superpower when channeled into advocating for your child's needs.[4]

Karen, another mom in my support group, discovered this firsthand. After years of beating herself up about her 'scattered' approach to parenting, she realized her ability to think outside the box helped her create unique solutions for her son's homework struggles. "My brain might not work like other moms," she shared, "but that's exactly why I could see solutions they couldn't."

Understanding our brain's neuroscience isn't about finding excuses; it's about finding explanations that lead to better solutions.[2] When we know why we struggle with certain tasks, we can develop strategies that work with our natural tendencies rather than against them.

For example, if traditional planning methods leave you feeling overwhelmed, try breaking tasks into smaller, more manageable chunks. Instead of writing "clean house" on your to-do list, break it down into specific, achievable tasks like "wipe kitchen counters" or "sort one drawer." This approach works better with our brain's reward system, giving us those small wins we need to maintain momentum.[3, 4]

Remember, your ADHD brain isn't broken; it's differently wired.[2] And that difference can be your greatest strength in navigating the complex journey of motherhood. The key isn't trying to think like everyone else; it's learning to work with your unique neural pathways to create systems and solutions that actually work for you and your family.[2, 4]

From Chaos to Creativity: Reframing ADHD Traits as Superpowers

Sarah stared at her kitchen counter, her heart racing as she surveyed the morning's chaos. Coffee steam mingled with the scent of slightly burnt toast while her children's backpacks gaped open nearby, waiting to be filled. The mental fog that often accompanied her ADHD made the pile of papers before her swim in and out of focus. Permission slips, birthday party invitations, and three different to-do lists competed for her attention. Her fingers drummed an anxious rhythm on the counter as she fought the urge to abandon the mess and retreat to the quiet of her car.[2]

But something felt different this morning. Instead of surrendering to the familiar wave of shame, Sarah remembered what her ADHD coach had told her last week: "Your creative chaos isn't a flaw - it's fuel for innovation." Taking a deep breath, she looked at the scattered papers with fresh eyes.[2]

I know this moment intimately because I've lived it countless times. Like Sarah, I've struggled to embrace my ADHD traits as strengths rather than stumbling blocks.[2] But I've discovered that our supposedly challenging traits often hide unexpected gifts.

Let me share what Rachel, one of the moms in my support group, discovered about her ADHD brain's tendency to make unexpected connections. "I used to beat myself up about getting distracted during my son's homework time," she told me. "Then one evening, while helping him with a particularly challenging math problem, my 'scattered' thinking helped me create a silly story that made the concept click for him. His teacher later asked to share my method with other students."[2, 5]

Our ADHD brains offer unique advantages in parenting:

That racing mind that seems to bounce from thought to thought? It helps us generate creative solutions when our kids face obstacles.[4] Last week, I turned a morning meltdown over mismatched socks into an impromptu lesson about embracing differences, all because my brain made a split-second connection between socks and acceptance.

Our intense emotions and empathy, often seen as overwhelming, allow us to tune into our children's feelings with remarkable precision.[5] Katie, another mom in our group, described how her emotional sensitivity helped her notice her daughter's anxiety about school long before it became obvious to others.

Even our tendency to hyperfocus, which can sometimes derail our daily plans, becomes a superpower when channeled into advocating for our children's needs or creating engaging learning experiences.[4] I once spent six hours developing an elaborate treasure hunt to teach my daughter multiplication tables; not conventional, but incredibly effective.

Maria discovered this truth during a parent-teacher conference. Apologizing for her unconventional approach to helping with homework, she was surprised when the teacher praised her creative methods. "Your son is thriving because you think differently," the teacher said. "He's learning there's more than one way to solve problems."[2, 5]

The key to transforming our ADHD traits into parenting strengths lies in acceptance and adaptation.[2] Instead of fighting against our unique brain wiring, we'll learn to harness it. When we embrace our different ways of thinking, we give our children an invaluable gift: the understanding that diversity in thought and approach enriches life.

Lisa struggled with traditional bedtime routines until she stopped trying to follow parenting books and created her own system. Now, bedtime involves storytelling, creative movement, and what she calls 'peaceful chaos,' a routine that honors both her ADHD energy and her children's need for wind-down time.[4]

Your ADHD traits aren't obstacles to overcome; they're unique tools waiting to be unleashed.[2] Together, we'll explore how to transform each challenging characteristic into a parenting superpower, creating a home environment where creativity flourishes and differences are celebrated.

Building Your Support System: Creating a Network That Gets You

Kerry's hands trembled as she gripped her steering wheel, tears threatening to spill onto her cheeks. The familiar wave of isolation washed over her as she sat in the school parking lot, watching other moms chat effortlessly in their perfectly coordinated workout gear. Her phone buzzed with another message from the class parent group; something about teacher appreciation week that she'd completely forgotten. Again. The sharp sting of failure felt like a physical pain in her chest.

I know this feeling intimately. Like Kerry, I've spent countless moments feeling like the odd mom out, struggling to keep up with the seemingly effortless juggling act other mothers appeared to master. But here's what I've learned: building a support system when you have ADHD isn't about fitting into the neurotypical mold; it's about finding your tribe of people who truly get you.[6]

Let me tell you about Molly, who transformed her parenting journey by taking one brave step. After months of isolating herself, afraid that other parents would judge her forgetfulness and chronic lateness, she finally reached out to an online ADHD parents' group. "The first time I posted about finding my kid's homework in the freezer," she told me, "instead of judgment, I got thirty responses from moms who'd done similar things. I cried for an hour; happy tears this time."

Your support system needs to be as unique as your ADHD brain. Rachel, another mom in my group, discovered this when she stopped trying to join traditional mommy groups and instead created what she calls her "chaos crew," a small circle of neurodivergent moms who meet for weekly coffee dates where showing up in mismatched socks is perfectly acceptable.

Building your network starts with honesty, both with yourself and others. When Emma finally opened up to her son's teacher about her ADHD struggles, she found an unexpected ally who helped create a communication system that worked for her brain. Instead of drowning in endless emails, they set up quick voice message `check-ins that actually got answered.

Here's what I've learned about creating a support system that truly works:

Start with your inner circle. Look for people who celebrate your creativity and problem-solving skills rather than trying to "fix" you.[6] Katie found her first real supporter in a neighbor who never judged her for forgetting garbage day but instead started texting gentle reminders.

Expand to professional support. An ADHD coach, therapist, or organizer who understands neurodivergent brains can provide invaluable strategies and validation.[6] Jane credits her ADHD coach with helping her transform from feeling like a "mom failure" to seeing her unique strengths.

Connect digitally with purpose. Online ADHD parent groups can be lifelines, especially during those 3 AM moments when you're organizing the pantry because sleep won't come. But choose your online spaces carefully; look for groups that focus on support and solutions rather than just venting.[6]

Build practical support networks. Exchange skills with other parents based on your natural strengths.[6,7] Amanda, who struggles with routine tasks but excels at creative projects, swaps help with another mom; trading birthday party planning for help with weekly meal prep.

Your support system should feel like a warm hug, not another item on your to-do list. It's okay to start small. Sometimes, one understanding friend who gets why you might text them five times about the same playdate is worth more than a dozen casual acquaintances.

Remember, you're not just building a network; you're creating a community where your ADHD traits are understood as unique features of who you are, not flaws to be fixed.[6] When Michelle joined our local ADHD moms' group, she said something that stuck with me: "For the first time, I don't have to explain why I showed up with my shirt inside out. These women just get it, and they love me anyway."

Your perfect support system might look messy to others, but that's exactly what makes it perfect for you. Start today by reaching out to just one person who might understand your journey; you might be surprised to find they've been waiting for someone like you, too.[6]

As we conclude this journey through understanding and embracing our ADHD motherhood, let's pause to celebrate how far we've come. Remember that morning when Sarah sat at her kitchen counter, surrounded by half-finished to-do lists and scattered sticky notes? Now she leads her local ADHD moms' support group, teaching others how to transform their challenges into strengths.

We've explored the unique gifts our ADHD brains bring to parenting, from Jennifer's innovative voice-note shopping system to Rachel's creative homework solutions. We've seen how our tendency to think differently isn't a flaw but a feature that helps us solve problems in ways that surprise and delight our children.

The path from viewing our ADHD as a deficit to recognizing it as a different way of experiencing the world isn't always smooth. There will still be days when we find our keys in the freezer or realize we've double-booked ourselves for three different activities. But now we understand that these moments don't define us; they're simply part of our unique motherhood story.

Your different is your children's normal. Your creative solutions, your emotional sensitivity, your ability to think outside the box; these aren't just coping mechanisms, they're valuable gifts you're passing on to your children. When you openly navigate life with ADHD, you're teaching them invaluable lessons about self-acceptance, resilience, and the beauty of neurodiversity.

As we move forward into exploring practical strategies in the next chapter, hold onto this truth: you're not just surviving motherhood with ADHD; you're blazing a trail for other mothers who might be feeling alone in their struggles. You're showing them that success doesn't look like fitting into a neurotypical mold; it looks like creating your own path.

Remember Maria's words from our support group last month? "The day I stopped apologizing for my ADHD and started working with it was the day I became the mother my children actually needed." She's right. Being a 'good mom' isn't about being perfect; it's about being authentically you, ADHD and all.

So the next time you find yourself about to apologize for your ADHD traits, pause and consider: What if these aren't bugs in your operating system, but features? What if your unique way of moving through the world is exactly what your family needs? Because here's the truth: you're not just making it work, you're showing others how to embrace their own neurodivergent journey, one creative solution at a time.

In the chapters ahead, we'll dive into practical strategies and systems that work with your ADHD brain rather than against it. But for now, take a moment to acknowledge how far you've come. You're doing more than surviving; you're redefining what successful motherhood looks like, and that's something worth celebrating.

Chapter 2:

Kitchen Table Command Center: Simple Systems for Household Chaos Control

If you're nodding along right now, quietly muttering "me too" under your breath, know that you're not alone in this beautiful mess of ADHD motherhood. Like many of us, I've learned that the path to managing our differently-wired brains isn't about becoming a different person; it's about discovering ways to work with our unique strengths rather than against them.

Motherhood with ADHD can feel like trying to conduct an orchestra while simultaneously learning to play each instrument. Some days, we're creating beautiful symphonies of organized chaos; other days, it's more like a toddler's first drum solo. But here's the thing: both are perfectly valid performances in the grand concert of parenting.

Sarah's story resonates with so many of us because it captures that pivotal moment when we realize our ADHD isn't something to overcome; it's something to understand and embrace. Her journey from tears in the car to finding creative solutions represents the heart of what this chapter is about: transforming our perceived weaknesses into unique parenting strengths.

In the pages that follow, we'll explore how to make your kitchen table your command center, with simple systems for household chaos control. We'll look at setting up a visual command centre, paper taming techniques, and how to time block and set up family routines.

As we dive deeper into this journey together, remember that your ADHD brain isn't a barrier to being a good mother; it's part of what makes you the exact mother your children need. When you learn to embrace your neurodivergent perspective, you'll discover that those very traits you've been trying to overcome might just be your greatest parenting superpowers.

Think about it: who better to teach children about thinking outside the box than a mom whose brain naturally colors outside the lines? Who better to model resilience than someone who navigates daily challenges with creativity and determination? Your ADHD isn't just part of your story; it's a vital chapter in your children's story too.

The Visual Command Center: Setting Up Your Kitchen Table Hub

I stared at my kitchen table, barely visible under the mountain of permission slips, birthday party invitations, bills, and at least three different to-do lists I'd started but never finished. Somewhere in that paper jungle was my daughter's field trip form (due tomorrow), my son's soccer schedule, and probably that water bill I couldn't remember if I'd paid. The sight made me want to grab my keys and escape to the nearest coffee shop.

But instead, I took a deep breath and remembered what my friend Kate, another ADHD mom, had taught me about "zones of control." The kitchen table, she explained, wasn't just a flat surface for collecting clutter; it could become the command center my ADHD brain desperately needed.[3]

That afternoon, I cleared everything off the table and started fresh. Rather than creating complicated categories that I'd never maintain,[1] I set up three simple stations: an action station (with a clear file holder for immediate needs), a family calendar station (with a large whiteboard), and a processing station (with clearly labeled folders). I hung a magnetic strip on the wall for incoming papers and added a charging station for our devices.

The transformation wasn't instant, but it was profound. Two weeks later, when I immediately knew where to find my son's soccer schedule and had submitted my daughter's permission slip on time, I realized this wasn't just about organization; it was about creating peace of mind.

The key was making everything visible. Our ADHD brains tend to follow the "out of sight, out of mind" rule religiously,[1, 3] so I made sure everything important stayed in plain sight. The whiteboard became our family's visual brain, tracking appointments, chores, and important reminders. The action station, with its clear folders, meant I could see at a glance what needed my attention.

I learned to attach new habits to existing routines; checking the action station while my morning coffee brewed, updating the whiteboard during dinner cleanup.[3] These weren't grand organizational schemes; they were simple, sustainable practices that worked with my ADHD brain instead of against it.

My friend Wendy, who struggled with paper overwhelm like I did, adapted this system for her smaller kitchen by using the inside of her cabinet doors. "I installed clear pockets on the doors," she told me, "and now every paper has a home that I can actually see when I need it."

The most surprising benefit wasn't just better organization; it was the ripple effect throughout our home. My kids knew where to put their school forms, my husband could easily check our family calendar, and I felt less anxious about missing important deadlines.[1] The kitchen table had become more than just a place to eat; it was now the heart of our family's organization system.

Remember, your command center doesn't need to look Instagram-perfect. Mine certainly doesn't. What matters is that it works for your brain and your family's needs.[2,3] Start small; maybe just with a calendar and an action folder. Add components as you get comfortable with the system. The goal isn't perfection; it's progress.

And on those days when papers still pile up (because they will), or when you find a permission slip that somehow escaped the system (because it happens), be gentle with yourself. A command center isn't about eliminating chaos completely; it's about creating a home base that helps you navigate the beautiful mess of ADHD motherhood with more confidence and less stress.[1,2,3]

Paper Taming Techniques: From Chaos to Clarity

I found my daughter's missing permission slip in the fruit bowl this morning, right next to last week's unpaid electric bill and a birthday party invitation that was probably due last month. Standing there, surrounded by paper chaos, I felt that familiar wave of shame wash over me; the one that hits every ADHD mom when her paper management system (or lack thereof) reaches critical mass.[2]

My kitchen counter looked like a paper tornado had swept through; school newsletters competed for space with grocery receipts, while important medical forms played hide-and-seek under junk mail. I'd tried every organizational system out there: color-coded folders that lost their meaning by day two, elaborate filing systems that became paper purgatory, and countless apps that promised digital salvation but just added another layer of complexity to my already overwhelmed brain.[3, 4]

It wasn't until I reached my breaking point, missing my son's field trip deadline because the form had become an impromptu coaster, that I finally discovered a system that worked with my ADHD brain instead of against it. The secret wasn't in creating more complicated systems; it was in simplifying and making everything visible[3].

I started with what I call the "Three-Tray Truth": one tray for immediate action items (things due this week), one for reference materials (stuff we need to keep handy but isn't urgent), and one for items to be filed away.[3] The key was placing these trays where I couldn't ignore them; right on my kitchen counter, next to the coffee maker. Because let's be honest, if it's not in my line of sight during my morning coffee ritual, it might as well be on Mars.

Next came what I like to call the "Daily Paper Patrol," a five-minute ritual tied to something I already do consistently (in my case, waiting for my coffee to brew). Each morning, I quickly sort any new papers into the appropriate trays. No lengthy decision-making process, no elaborate filing system; just quick triage to keep the paper flow moving.[3]

The game-changer was creating a "Command Center Wall" next to our kitchen table. I installed a large magnetic whiteboard with clear pockets for active papers, a family calendar, and a "This Week Matters" section for time-sensitive items.[5] Everything important stayed visible, and the magnetic surface meant I could quickly post new items without having to find a perfect home for them.

My friend Jessica, another ADHD mom, adapted this system by using the inside of her cabinet doors, creating what she calls her "Paper Portal," clear pockets mounted inside the doors where she can easily see and access important documents while keeping her counters clear.[5]

The most liberating part of this system is its forgiveness. Papers still sometimes end up in weird places (I recently found a bank statement bookmarking my cookbook), but now I have a simple way to get them back on track. It's not about perfect organization; it's about creating a system that catches us when we inevitably stumble.[3]

For those really important papers, the ones that would cause major headaches if lost, I immediately take a photo with my phone and add it to a dedicated "Important Papers" album. This digital backup has saved me more times than I can count, especially when papers mysteriously migrate to unexpected locations (like that time I found my son's immunization records in the freezer; don't ask).[3]

Remember, the goal isn't to transform into a perfectly organized paper manager overnight. It's about creating simple, sustainable systems that work with your ADHD brain rather than against it.[3, 4] Start small, maybe just with the three-tray system, and build from there as each piece becomes habitual.

My kitchen counter still isn't going to win any organizational awards, but now when I need to find that permission slip or important bill, I know exactly where to look. And more importantly, I've stopped beating myself up about not being naturally organized.[2] Because sometimes the best systems aren't the ones that look the prettiest; they're the ones that actually work for our beautifully chaotic ADHD brains.

Time Blocking and Family Routines: Making the System Stick

I stood in my kitchen, staring at the clock that seemed to mock me as I juggled three different morning tasks at once. My daughter needed help finding her soccer cleats, my son was still eating breakfast fifteen minutes after we should have left, and I had a work meeting in exactly twenty-seven minutes. Time, that elusive concept that neurotypical people seemed to grasp so naturally, was once again slipping through my fingers like water.[6, 7]

It wasn't until I found myself making lunch at 10 PM while simultaneously trying to fold laundry and answer work emails that I realized something had to change. My attempts at time management felt like trying to catch butterflies with a fishing net; technically possible, but definitely not the right tool for the job.[6]

That's when Caitlin, my friend from the ADHD support group, introduced me to time blocking, but not the rigid, every-minute-scheduled kind that had failed me countless times before. "Think of it like building with Lego blocks," she explained, "You start with the big pieces, the non-negotiables like school drop-off and bedtime, and then add the smaller blocks around them."[6]

I started simple, creating what I call my "anchor points" throughout the day. Instead of trying to schedule every minute, I identified key transition moments: morning launch (7-8 AM), after-school reset (3-4 PM), and evening wind-down (7-8 PM). These became my daily cornerstones, the reliable pillars around which everything else could flex and flow.[6]

The magic happened when I made these blocks visual. I hung a large whiteboard in our kitchen, using different colors for each family member. But here's the crucial part: I left white space. Lots of it. My ADHD brain needs room to breathe, to accommodate the inevitable unexpected tasks and time blindness that comes with our unique wiring.[6]

I learned to build in what I call "buffer bubbles," those extra pockets of time that account for my tendency to underestimate how long tasks take. Getting ready for school doesn't take 20 minutes; it takes 35 when you factor in the lost shoe, the last-minute permission slip signing, and the inevitable "I forgot to..." moment.[6]

The game-changer came when I started involving my kids in the process. Every Sunday evening, we have what we call our "Week Preview," a 15-minute family meeting where we review the coming week's schedule together. My daughter color-codes her activities, my son adds stickers to his important days, and suddenly, time management became a family project rather than Mom's futile attempt at organizing chaos.[6]

But let's be real; some days, the system falls apart. There are mornings when we're running late despite every carefully placed block, afternoons when activities overlap in impossible ways, and evenings when dinner happens at bizarre hours. The difference now is that we have a framework to return to, a familiar rhythm that helps us reset rather than spiral.[6]

I've learned that successful time blocking for ADHD families isn't about perfect adherence to a schedule. It's about creating a flexible structure that can bend without breaking. We use phrases like "it's almost red block time" (our code for bedtime routine) or "we're in the yellow zone" (homework and snack time) to help everyone stay oriented without feeling constrained.[6]

One of my favorite tools is what I call the "time anchor checklist," not a rigid schedule, but a simple list of what needs to happen during each block. For our morning block, it's: medication, breakfast, dressed, teeth, and backpack. The order can vary, but seeing these tasks grouped together helps my ADHD brain stay on track without feeling overwhelmed by time pressure.[6]

Remember, the goal isn't to suddenly become a time management guru. It's about creating a system that catches you when you fall off track and helps you find your way back. Start small, maybe just with one solid morning or evening routine, and build from there. Your time blocks should feel like friendly guides, not prison walls.[6]

As another ADHD mom in my support group likes to say, "We're not aiming for perfect time management. We're aiming for 'good enough' time management that gets us through the day with our sanity intact."[6, 7] And sometimes, that's the biggest victory of all.

I'm staring at my kitchen table right now, buried under a week's worth of school papers, half-finished to-do lists, and that permission slip I swear I signed but somehow never made it back to school. This scene, this beautiful mess, represents exactly where many of us ADHD moms find ourselves daily. But here's what I've learned: this chaos isn't a sign of failure; it's an opportunity for transformation.

Through this chapter, we've explored how our ADHD brains aren't broken; they're differently wired in ways that can actually enhance our parenting journey. We've seen how Jenny transformed her overwhelming paper piles into a functional Family Command Wall, how Sarah turned her car-crying moments into community-building opportunities, and how countless other moms have discovered that working with their ADHD traits rather than against them creates sustainable success.

The kitchen table chaos that once triggered shame can become a launching pad for creative solutions. Those sticky notes scattered everywhere? They can evolve into a visual planning system that actually works with our "out of sight, out of mind" tendencies. That pile of unfinished projects? It's evidence of our ability to think outside the box and see possibilities others might miss.

What I've discovered, and what I hope you're beginning to see, is that embracing our neurodivergent motherhood doesn't mean settling for chaos. It means recognizing that our path to organization and success might look different from the traditional parenting playbook, and that's perfectly okay. When we stop fighting our natural tendencies and start channeling them constructively, we create systems that not only work for us but also teach our children valuable lessons about adaptability and self-acceptance.

The strategies we've explored, from creating visible organization systems to building support networks that understand ADHD challenges, aren't just about managing our daily lives. They're about transforming our perceived weaknesses into unique parenting strengths. Every time we model resilience in the face of challenges or demonstrate creative problem-solving, we're showing our children that different doesn't mean deficient.

As we move forward to the next chapter, where we'll dive deeper into having a mind like a browser with 100 tabs open, carry this truth with you: Your ADHD brain isn't something to overcome; it's a unique lens through which you view and interact with the world, offering your children perspectives and possibilities they might not otherwise see. Your journey isn't about becoming a different kind of mother; it's about becoming the best version of the mother you already are.

Remember that those times of finding homework in the freezer can lead to creating a system that not only works for an ADHD brain but can also teach your children valuable lessons about adaptability and creative problem-solving. These are the moments that transform our challenges into opportunities for growth and connection.

You're not just surviving motherhood with ADHD; you're pioneering a path for other mothers who might be feeling alone in their struggles. Keep experimenting, keep adapting, and most importantly, keep embracing your perfectly imperfect ADHD mom journey. Because sometimes the most beautiful symphonies come from those who dare to play their instruments differently.

Chapter 3:

Mind Like a Browser with 100 Tabs Open: Managing the Mental Load of Motherhood

Motherhood is a constant juggling act. For moms with ADHD, it can feel more like trying to juggle flaming torches while balancing on a moving train. The mind races, tabs multiply, and every thought seems equally urgent: right down to remembering snack day, replying to that school email, and ordering more laundry detergent. It's no wonder the mental load can start to feel like an overflowing inbox with no clear way to hit "sort."

This chapter explores how to bring some order to that inner chaos. We'll begin with Digital Brain Dumping, using technology as a supportive ally to capture the storm of thoughts before they slip away. Then we shift to Task Triage, learning how to separate what's truly urgent from what only feels that way when everything's demanding attention at once. Finally, we'll move into Creating Mental Bandwidth, with practical strategies to lighten the load, reclaim focus, and make mental space for what really matters.

By the end of this chapter, you'll have a toolkit to help close a few of those mental tabs, and perhaps, for the first time in a while, breathe deeply and say, "Okay. I've got this."

Digital Brain Dumping: Using Technology to Capture the Mental Load

Picture this: You're stirring pasta for dinner while mentally rehearsing tomorrow's work presentation, trying to remember if you signed that permission slip, and suddenly remembering you need to schedule a dentist appointment; all while your phone pings with texts from the school's parent group. Sound familiar? For ADHD moms, this mental juggling act isn't just occasional; it's our daily reality.[2]

I remember the day I found my daughter's birthday party invitations in the freezer, right next to the grocery list I'd been searching for all week. That was my breaking point; the moment I realized I needed a better system than trying to keep everything in my overloaded brain. Like many ADHD moms, my mind felt like a web browser with countless tabs open, each one threatening to crash my mental operating system at any moment.[1, 2]

This is where technology becomes our secret weapon. Think of your smartphone as a second brain, one that never gets overwhelmed or forgets where it put things.[1] When Sasha, a mom from my ADHD support group, showed me how she'd transformed her phone into her external memory system, it was like watching someone perform magic. "I used to have sticky notes everywhere," she told me, "but now everything goes straight into my phone the moment it pops into my head."

The key is capturing thoughts and tasks the moment they appear, using whatever method feels most natural. For Sasha, it's voice notes recorded while driving: her brilliant ideas for work projects, reminders about school supplies, or that perfect solution for organizing the garage she thought of at a red light. Another mom I know swears by taking photos of important documents instead of trying to file them, while I've found that quick text notes work best for my brain.[1,2]

But here's the most important thing I've learned: your digital system doesn't need to be perfect or complicated. Start simple. Your phone's built-in notes app might be all you need at first. The goal isn't to create an elaborate organizational masterpiece; it's to free up mental space so you can focus on what truly matters, like being present with your children or tackling that creative project you've been dreaming about.[1]

I've watched countless ADHD moms transform their daily experience by embracing digital tools. Like Abigail, who finally stopped missing important school events after setting up a shared family calendar with automated reminders. Or Cathy, who reduced her morning chaos by using a simple checklist app that both she and her kids could access.[1,2]

The beauty of digital brain dumping is that it works with our ADHD tendencies rather than against them. Those random thoughts that pop up while we're washing dishes? Capture them with a quick voice note. That brilliant idea that strikes during the school pickup line? Type it into your phone before it vanishes. Your digital tools become a trusted partner in managing the mental load, always ready to catch those important thoughts before they slip away.[1]

Start by noticing when you feel most overwhelmed; maybe it's during the morning rush, or perhaps in the evening when tomorrow's tasks start crowding your mind. These are your cues to do a quick digital brain dump. Open your chosen app and let the thoughts flow out, knowing they'll be there waiting when you need them. Over time, this simple practice can transform the way you manage your mental load, turning that overwhelming browser with too many tabs into an organized, searchable system that works for you.[1, 2]

Task Triage: Prioritizing When Everything Feels Urgent

It's 7:43 AM, and I'm standing in my kitchen staring at three permission slips that need signing, a stack of unopened mail, my laptop open to an urgent work email, and my daughter asking if I've ordered her science project supplies yet. My phone buzzes with a text from the PTA about volunteers needed for next week's event, and I can feel my heart racing as every task screams for immediate attention. This is the reality of being an ADHD mom; when everything feels urgent, how do we decide what truly needs our attention right now?[1, 3]

I remember sitting with my friend Rachel during one of these overwhelming moments, watching tears well up in her eyes as she whispered, "I don't even know where to start anymore." That's when I shared with her what my ADHD coach had taught me about task triage: a way of sorting through the chaos that actually works with our unique brain wiring instead of against it.[3]

Think of task triage like an emergency room nurse; they don't treat every patient simultaneously, even though each person needs care. They assess, prioritize, and act accordingly. For ADHD moms, this means learning to distinguish between what feels urgent and what truly is urgent.[3]

Lisa, a mom from my support group, transformed her approach to daily tasks after a particularly overwhelming Monday morning. "I used to panic about everything: unmade beds, unfolded laundry, unanswered emails, all competing for attention in my mind," she shared. "Now I ask myself three simple questions: Will there be serious consequences if this doesn't get done today? Is there a real, time-sensitive deadline? Does this directly impact my family's well-being?"[1]

These questions became Lisa's lifeline, helping her brain shift from panic mode to purposeful action. She started using colored sticky notes on her kitchen wall: red for truly urgent tasks (like signing that permission slip due tomorrow), yellow for important but not immediate needs (like scheduling a routine dentist check-up), and green for everything else (like organizing the garage). Within weeks, she found herself naturally gravitating toward the red tasks first, while feeling less guilty about the green ones that could wait.[1]

Jackie, another mom in our group, adapted this system for her digital planner. "I used to have fifty reminders set for each day, all marked as high priority," she laughed. "Now I understand that while the dishes might need doing today because they affect our ability to cook dinner, the unfolded laundry can probably wait until tomorrow without any real consequences."[1]

The beauty of task triage isn't just in helping us decide what to do first; it's in permitting us to let some things wait. Angela, a working mom of three, found freedom in this realization. "I always felt like I was failing because I couldn't get everything done immediately," she shared. "Understanding task triage helped me see that it's not about doing everything; it's about doing the right things at the right time."[1,3]

Start small; choose one overwhelming area of your life and apply the three questions. Maybe it's your email inbox, or that stack of papers on your kitchen counter. As you practice, you'll find yourself developing an intuition for true urgency versus perceived urgency. Share this approach with your family, too. Even young children can learn to understand the difference between red, yellow, and green tasks, helping them develop their own prioritization skills while understanding why mom might say "not right now" to certain requests.[1]

Remember, the goal isn't perfection; it's progress. Some days, you might only get to the red flag items, and that's okay. Other days, you might surprise yourself by tackling some yellow or green tasks too. What matters is having a system that helps you focus your attention where it's needed most, reducing that overwhelming feeling that everything must be done right now.[3]

As Lisa told me recently, "Task triage didn't just change how I manage my to-do list - it changed how I see myself as a mom. I'm not failing when I can't do everything at once. I'm succeeding by doing the most important things first."[1, 3]

Creating Mental Bandwidth: Strategies for Clearing Mental Clutter

Ruth stood in her kitchen, surrounded by the morning chaos of breakfast dishes, backpacks, and permission slips, when she suddenly realized she couldn't remember if she'd taken her medication. Was it this morning? Yesterday? Her brain felt like a computer with too many programs running simultaneously, each demanding immediate attention. The mental fog was so thick she could almost see it.[3, 2]

This overwhelming mental clutter is a daily reality for many ADHD moms. We're constantly juggling schedules, remembering medication times, tracking appointments, and maintaining mental checklists for every family member; all while trying to focus on the immediate task at hand.[2] It's exhausting, and sometimes it feels impossible to create the mental bandwidth we desperately need.

I remember sitting with Kate, a mom from my ADHD support group, as she described her mental state: "It's like having fifty browser tabs open in my brain, and they're all playing videos at full volume." Her description perfectly captured that feeling of mental overwhelm that so many of us experience.[3, 2]

But here's what I've learned: creating mental bandwidth isn't about achieving perfect focus or complete mental quiet. It's about finding practical ways to reduce the cognitive noise so we can think more clearly.[2] For instance, Emily, another mom in our group, transformed her daily experience by creating what she calls her "mental reset spaces" throughout her house. She placed small notepads in key locations, by her bed, near the coffee maker, in her car, to capture thoughts the moment they arise instead of letting them bounce around in her head.

The most powerful shift often comes from permitting ourselves to externalize our mental load. Rachel discovered this when she finally stopped trying to remember everything and started using her phone's voice notes feature. "I used to feel guilty about not being able to keep it all in my head," she shared. "Now I understand that my brain works better when I give it the support it needs."[3]

Creating mental bandwidth also means learning to recognize when we're approaching overload. Mia, a working mom of three, developed what she calls her "traffic light system." When she notices she's starting to feel scattered, she takes a moment to close her eyes, take three deep breaths, and mentally sort her thoughts into three categories: urgent (red), important but not immediate (yellow), and can wait (green). This simple practice helps her brain shift from panic mode to purposeful action.[2]

One of the most effective strategies I've discovered is what I call the "mental declutter routine." Each evening, I spend five minutes writing down everything that's taking up space in my mind, from grocery lists to work projects to worries about my kids. As these thoughts transfer from my head to paper, I can physically feel my mental bandwidth expanding. It's like closing unnecessary programs to free up processing power.[3, 2]

The key is finding what works for your unique brain. Maybe it's using a digital task manager that syncs across all your devices, or perhaps it's a simple notebook that lives on your kitchen counter. The goal isn't to eliminate mental clutter entirely; that's neither realistic nor necessary. Instead, we're aiming to create enough mental space to think clearly and respond intentionally to what's happening in the present moment.[2]

Remember, your ADHD brain isn't broken; it just processes information differently.[3] When we build systems that work with our natural tendencies rather than against them, we can create the mental bandwidth we need to navigate motherhood with greater ease and confidence. As Kate told me during our last coffee date, "I still have lots of tabs open in my brain, but now I know how to mute the ones that aren't serving me right now."[3, 2]

Standing in your kitchen, surrounded by the daily evidence of family life, permission slips waiting to be signed, grocery lists needing attention, and calendar notifications competing for your focus, you might wonder if creating an organized command center is really possible with your ADHD brain. Let me assure you: not only is it possible, but you're already halfway there simply by recognizing the need for a system that works with your unique way of thinking.

Through this chapter, we've explored how your mind can feel like a browser with 100 tabs open.

The strategies we've discussed, from digital brain dumping to task triage and creating mental whitespace, are more than just organizational tools. They're pathways to reducing that overwhelming mental load that so many ADHD moms carry. When Ellen first implemented her morning "tab-closing routine," she found herself not just more organized but more present with her children, able to focus on their stories rather than the swirling to-do lists in her mind.

Remember that progress isn't linear. Some days, your system will work flawlessly; other days, you might find permission slips in the fruit bowl again. That's okay. What matters is that you're building a foundation for better organization, one that honors your ADHD brain while supporting your family's needs.

Celebrate the small victories along the way: when you find that important paper right where it should be, when your children naturally adopt the new systems you've put in place, or when you finally remember to sign and return that field trip form on time. These moments aren't just wins for organization; they're steps toward a more peaceful, functioning household that works with, rather than against, your unique way of thinking.

As we move forward, carry with you the knowledge that your kitchen table is now more than just a place for meals; it's the heart of your family's organization system, a physical reminder that ADHD doesn't have to mean chaos. Your command center, whether simple or elaborate, is a testament to your commitment to creating order in a way that makes sense for you and your family.

In the next chapter, we'll build on these foundations as we explore more strategies for creating routines that stick so you can move from scattered to structured. But for now, take a moment to appreciate how far you've come. You are able to use technology as a digital brain dump, triage tasks, and create mental bandwidth.

Chapter 4:

From Scattered to Structured: Creating Routines That Actually Stick (No, Really!)

As I work with ADHD moms in my support groups, I've noticed that our kitchen tables often become more than just eating spaces; they transform into the heart of our family organization systems, whether we plan it that way or not. It's where permission slips pile up, where homework happens, and where we attempt to sort through the endless stream of daily life.

The truth is, for ADHD moms, traditional organization methods often feel like trying to fit a square peg into a round hole. We need systems that work with our visual nature and our need for immediate accessibility. That's why the kitchen table command center concept has become such a game-changer for many of us.

Take Debra's story, for example. Her kitchen table was drowning in papers: school permission slips, birthday party invitations, bills, and multiple unfinished to-do lists. Her daughter needed a check for the field trip tomorrow, her son's soccer schedule was buried somewhere in the pile, and she couldn't remember if she'd paid the water bill. The sight of it all made her want to grab her keys and escape to the nearest coffee shop. Instead, she took a deep breath and remembered what her friend Sal, another ADHD mom, had told her about 'zones of control.'

That afternoon, Debra cleared everything off the table and created three simple stations: an action station with a clear file holder for immediate needs, a family calendar station with a large whiteboard, and a processing station with labeled folders. She hung a magnetic strip on the wall for incoming papers and added a charging station for devices. Two weeks later, when she immediately knew where to find her son's soccer schedule and had submitted her daughter's permission slip on time, Debra realized that this wasn't just about organization; it was about creating peace of mind.

In this chapter, we'll look at simple, sustainable systems that can help you manage the daily paper shuffle, create visual reminders that actually work, and establish routines that the whole family can follow. Most importantly, we'll focus on solutions that don't require you to completely change who you are or how your brain works.

Remember, the goal isn't to create a Pinterest-perfect organization system; it's to develop a practical, workable solution that helps you manage your family's needs while honoring your unique way of processing information. Let's dive in and discover how to make routines that stick and work with your unique brain, often by stacking habits on your existing ones so that they build and feel natural.

Building Flexible Routines: The ADHD-Friendly Framework

I stared at the elaborate morning routine chart taped to my bathroom mirror: color-coded, laminated, and filled with twenty-seven detailed steps that would supposedly transform my chaotic mornings into a well-oiled machine. It was the fourth such chart I'd created this year, and deep down, I knew it would likely join its predecessors in the drawer of abandoned organizational systems. Does this sound familiar?

For years, I believed I was failing at routines because I wasn't trying hard enough or wasn't disciplined enough. But here's what I've learned: it wasn't about effort or discipline; it was about trying to force my square-peg ADHD brain into round-hole traditional routines.[1]

The breakthrough came when I stopped attempting complete life overhauls and started building what I call "flexible frameworks," routines that bend without breaking.[1,2] Instead of that 27-step morning checklist, I began with just one small change: placing my medication and a glass of water on my nightstand the night before. After a week of successfully taking my medication first thing every morning, I felt ready to add another small step.

This is the approach that finally worked for me, and I've seen it work for countless other ADHD moms in my support groups. Take Jill, for example. She spent years beating herself up about her inability to maintain the elaborate after-school routine she thought she "should" have. Everything changed when she identified just three non-negotiable anchor points in her afternoon: snack time, homework start time, and dinner prep. Between these anchors, she allowed flexibility for how things got done.[1]

The key is understanding that ADHD-friendly routines look different from neurotypical ones. They need built-in flexibility, visual cues, and room for our natural tendency toward novelty.[1] When Rebecca, a mom from my support group, realized this, she transformed her evening routine by creating what she calls her "sunset signals," simple environmental cues that tell her brain it's time to transition. As the sun starts setting, she turns on specific lamps, plays certain music, and uses these natural cues to ease into her evening tasks.[1]

Here's what makes an ADHD-friendly routine actually stick: it starts small, builds gradually, and includes recovery plans for when things go sideways (because they will).[1,2] Instead of trying to overhaul your entire day, choose one small window of time; maybe just the first 30 minutes after you wake up. Identify the absolute essentials that need to happen in that time frame, then build simple, visual reminders to support those tasks.[1]

Amy struggled for years with morning chaos until she created what she calls her "coffee station launching pad." While her coffee brews (something she never forgets to do), she uses those three minutes to complete one small task: unloading the dishwasher, checking the calendar, or sorting through her kids' backpacks. This tiny routine, anchored to something she naturally does every day, became the foundation for a more organized morning.

The beauty of flexible frameworks is that they're designed to bend, not break.[1] When (not if) your routine gets disrupted, you don't have to start over from scratch. You can jump back in at your next anchor point, knowing that your framework is strong enough to handle life's inevitable curveballs.[2]

As you begin building your own flexible framework, remember: you're not trying to change who you are. You're creating a system that works with your unique brain wiring, not against it.[1] Start with one small change, celebrate your successes (no matter how tiny), and give yourself permission to adjust and adapt as needed.[2] After all, the most effective routine is one that you can actually maintain.

Transition Mastery: Smoothing the Rough Edges of Daily Life

Standing in my kitchen, staring at the clock while simultaneously trying to get my daughter to finish her breakfast, pack my son's lunch, and remember if I'd taken my medication, I felt that familiar overwhelm of transition time creeping in. My heart raced as I realized we had exactly seven minutes to get out the door, and somehow my keys had disappeared again. This is what transitions look like for many of us ADHD moms: moments of barely controlled chaos that can make or break our entire day.[3, 4]

I remember the day I finally broke down in tears after another failed attempt at getting everyone out the door on time. My friend Kendra, another ADHD mom, gently reminded me that my brain processes transitions differently, and that's okay. "We're not failing at transitions," she said, "we just need different strategies to navigate them."

The science behind why transitions are particularly challenging for ADHD brains has to do with our executive function; that mental gear-shifting mechanism that helps people smoothly move from one task to another.[3, 4] For us, it's like trying to drive a manual transmission car without ever being taught how to use the clutch. We know where we need to go, but the process of getting there can be jerky and frustrating.

Let me share what worked for Andrea, a mom in my support group. She struggled with the afternoon transition from work to home life until she created what she calls her "reset ritual." Before leaving her office, she takes five minutes to close her eyes, take three deep breaths, and mentally picture herself switching from work mode to mom mode. This simple practice has transformed her evening transitions from chaos to relative calm.

The key to mastering transitions isn't about forcing ourselves to follow neurotypical patterns; it's about creating bridges that work for our unique brains.[3] For instance, I've learned to create what I call "transition anchors," physical cues that signal my brain it's time to shift gears. My morning anchor is my coffee maker's timer; when it starts brewing, that's my cue to begin our getting-ready routine.

Zoe, another mom from our community, transformed her family's morning chaos by implementing what she calls "transition zones." She set up three distinct areas in her home: the "launching pad" by the door for shoes and bags, the "fuel station" in the kitchen for breakfast and medications, and the "gear check" zone in the hallway for backpack supplies.[5] Each zone has visual cues and everything needed for that part of the morning routine.

One of the most powerful lessons I've learned is that transitions don't have to be perfect to be effective. When Lois shared how she sometimes sits in her car for five minutes between errands, just to reset her brain before the next task, it reminded me that taking these small transition pauses isn't a sign of weakness; it's a strategy for success.[4]

Here's what I want you to remember: Your ADHD brain isn't broken; it just processes transitions differently.[3] Instead of fighting against this, we can work with it. Start by identifying your most challenging daily transitions. For many of us, it's the morning rush, the after-school chaos, or the bedtime wind-down. Then, create simple bridges between activities; maybe it's a special song that signals cleanup time, or a specific phrase that helps your children know it's time to switch gears.[5]

Remember Rebecca's story? She struggled with bedtime transitions until she created her "sunset sequence," a series of small, connected actions that guide her family toward bedtime. It starts with dimming specific lights, playing calm music, and using lavender lotion during story time. These sensory cues help her ADHD brain recognize and respond to the transition naturally, rather than fighting against it.

Transitions may never be our favorite part of the day, but they don't have to be our biggest source of stress either. By understanding and working with our unique brain wiring, we can create smooth pathways between activities that feel natural and supportive rather than forced and overwhelming.[3, 4] You're not alone in this journey; we're all learning to dance with transitions in our own way, one small step at a time.

The Power of Habit Stacking: Creating Sustainable Change

I stood in my kitchen, staring at the mountain of dishes in the sink while my daughter's backpack sat unopened on the counter, probably containing important forms I needed to sign. The familiar wave of overwhelm started to rise; I had tried and failed countless times to create routines that would prevent these evening pile-ups. Maybe you've been there too, telling yourself that tomorrow you'll finally get organized, tomorrow you'll start that perfect routine you've planned out in your head.

It wasn't until I discovered habit stacking that things began to change. Not overnight, and not perfectly, but gradually and sustainably.[1] The breakthrough came during a particularly chaotic evening when I found myself automatically checking my phone while waiting for my coffee to brew. That's when it hit me; I already had habits, they just weren't serving me well. What if I could piggyback new, helpful habits onto the things I already do without thinking?

Let me share Lottie's story, which might sound familiar. Every evening, she'd promise herself that tomorrow would be different; she'd check her kids' backpacks, prepare for the next day, and finally feel on top of things. But despite her best intentions, tomorrow would bring the same scattered rush.[1] Then she learned about habit stacking during one of our ADHD support group meetings. She started small, linking one new action to her existing coffee routine: while her coffee brewed, she would open her children's backpacks and check for forms. Just that one simple stack. Within weeks, she never missed another permission slip.

The magic of habit stacking for ADHD brains lies in its simplicity.[1] Instead of trying to build elaborate new routines from scratch, we attach small, manageable actions to things we already do automatically. Think about it; you probably don't have to remind yourself to brush your teeth or pour your morning coffee. These are your anchor habits, the reliable actions that happen regardless of how scattered you feel.

Rose, another mom from our group, transformed her mornings by stacking three simple habits onto her automatic coffee routine: while the coffee brews, she unloads the dishwasher. While it steeps, she reviews her calendar. While she drinks it, she makes her priority list for the day. "It's not about being perfect," she tells other moms. "It's about making one small connection at a time."

The key is starting small.[1] Choose one anchor habit, something you already do without thinking, and attach one new action to it. Maybe while you brush your teeth, you'll lay out tomorrow's clothes. Or while waiting for your kids to put on their shoes (something that happens every day, even if it takes forever!), you'll review your calendar.

Remember that by linking just one new habit to an evening teeth-brushing routine, such as laying out medication for the next day, you can achieve your goal. This single stack can create a ripple effect of positive changes to a morning routine. Rather than trying to transform your entire life overnight, you can build one small bridge at a time between who you were and who you want to be.

This approach works because it honors how ADHD brains function.[1] We're not fighting against our nature or trying to force ourselves into neurotypical patterns. We're simply connecting new behaviors to existing ones, creating a natural flow that feels less like a struggle and more like a dance.

The beauty of habit stacking is its flexibility.[1] When life inevitably throws us curveballs (as it always does), we haven't lost everything if one part slips. We can easily pick back up with our next anchor habit and continue building our stack.

I still remember standing in my kitchen, tears streaming down my face as I stared at the chaos covering every inch of my table. Permission slips, bills, school announcements, and at least four different to-do lists competed for space with yesterday's breakfast dishes. In that moment, I felt like I was failing at everything: as a mother, as a professional, and as an adult who should be able to handle basic organization. Maybe you've had a similar moment, wondering why something as simple as managing papers seems so impossibly hard.

But here's what I want you to know: Your struggles aren't a reflection of your capabilities as a mother. Your ADHD brain processes information differently, and traditional organization systems often work against your natural tendencies rather than with them. That's why creating a kitchen table command center that aligns with your unique needs is so transformative.

Think about the journey, from drowning in paper piles to developing a system that actually works for your family. The command center may not be Instagram-worthy, but it's functional. When you create clear zones that match your visual processing style, you will establish simple routines for handling incoming papers, and most importantly, permit yourself to adapt the system as needed.

As you move forward with creating your own command center, remember that progress isn't linear. Some days, your table might look perfectly organized, while on others it might revert to chaos. That's okay. What matters is that you're building a foundation for family organization that works with your unique way of thinking.

Caroline started with just three bins: Action Required, Reference, and File Away. It wasn't fancy, but it was a step forward. Six months later, she had refined her system to include a family calendar station, a homework zone, and a bill-paying area that actually helped her remember due dates. The key wasn't perfection; it was progress.

Your kitchen table command center is more than just an organization system; it's a physical representation of how you're learning to work with your ADHD brain instead of against it. Every labeled folder, every clear bin, every designated space is a step toward creating order in a way that makes sense for you.

As we move into the next chapter about juggling a career and family, carry this truth with you: You aren't broken, and you don't need fixing. You just need systems that support the wonderful, unique way your brain works. Your command center might not look like anyone else's, and that's exactly as it should be.

Remember, every time you return that permission slip on time, every time you find the bill before it's late, every time you help your child locate their homework without a frantic search; these are victories worth celebrating. You've got this, mama, one small step at a time.

Chapter 5:

Working Mom Wizardry: Juggling Career and Kids with an ADHD Brain

For busy mothers with ADHD, this constant mental juggling isn't just challenging; it's exhausting. The endless stream of tasks, appointments, and responsibilities can feel like a relentless browser refresh, with each new notification threatening to override important information already stored in our working memory.

Amanda's story resonates with so many of us who've experienced that overwhelming sensation of mental tabs multiplying faster than we can process them. Like her, we've sat at our desks, struggling to focus on work while our thoughts pinball between household tasks, children's needs, and countless other responsibilities. The beauty of her solution wasn't in creating a perfect system; it was in acknowledging her brain's natural tendencies and finding ways to work with them rather than against them.

In the whirlwind of deadlines, school drop-offs, and endless to-do lists, ADHD moms stand at the crossroads of brilliance and chaos, balancing demanding careers with the vibrant energy of family life. This chapter celebrates that juggling act, not as a struggle, but as a kind of wizardry: the art of transforming everyday overwhelm into organized momentum.

We'll explore how task switching can become a superpower rather than a source of stress, with strategies to move smoothly between work and home roles. We'll look at how to design an ADHD-friendly workspace that reflects both focus and flexibility. And finally, we'll dive into "calendar choreography," learning how to align professional goals and family rhythms so that your days feel less like conflict and more like harmony.

Whether you're managing projects at the office or mini-crises at home, these tools will help you approach both worlds with confidence, creativity, and a touch of magic.

Task Switching Mastery: Transitioning Between Work and Home Modes

I used to think I was just terrible at transitions until I realized my ADHD brain was simply processing these shifts differently.[3] The day I found myself simultaneously typing a work email while helping my daughter with homework, and doing neither particularly well, was my wake-up call. Like many ADHD moms, I struggled with the constant mental gear-shifting between work mode and home mode, often feeling like I wasn't fully present in either world.[1, 2]

The challenge isn't just about managing time; it's about managing our brain's energy and attention.[3] Our ADHD minds don't come with a convenient on-off switch between professional and parent mode. Instead, we often find ourselves mentally drafting work presentations during family dinner or remembering urgent parent-teacher meetings during important work calls.[1]

Annie, a marketing executive and mother of two, shared how she transformed her work-from-home experience by creating what she calls "mode switching stations." She set up a dedicated workspace in her bedroom for focused work time and designated the kitchen table as her family's command center. "When I'm at my desk, my family knows I'm in work mode. When I'm at the kitchen table, I'm in mom mode," she explains. "This physical boundary helped my brain understand which hat I was wearing at any given moment."

The key isn't trying to build impenetrable walls between our different roles; that's not realistic for any parent, let alone one with ADHD.[2] Instead, it's about creating gentle transitions that help our brains shift gears more smoothly. Think of it like having a mental changing room between activities rather than instantly teleporting from one role to another.[2]

Melissa, a freelance writer and single mom, discovered the power of transition rituals almost by accident. "I started using my car as a transition zone," she shares. "After work and before picking up my kids, I spend ten minutes in my parked car doing a quick meditation and reviewing my evening game plan. It sounds simple, but it's like hitting a reset button for my brain."[2]

What works for me is what I call my "shutdown sequence" - a series of small actions that signal to my brain it's time to switch modes.[3] When ending work time, I write down any lingering tasks, close my laptop with intention, and take a brief walk around the block. This physical ritual helps prevent work thoughts from bleeding into family time.

Technology can be either our best friend or worst enemy in maintaining these boundaries.[1] I learned to create different user profiles on my devices: one for work and one for family time. This simple step prevents work notifications from infiltrating family time and vice versa. It's not about achieving perfect separation; it's about creating enough structure to prevent complete chaos.

Remember, mastering transitions isn't about perfection; it's about progress.[2] Start small by choosing one transition point in your day to focus on. Maybe it's the shift from morning work to afternoon school pickup, or from dinner time to evening work catch-up. Create a simple ritual around this transition and practice it consistently. You'll likely find that even small changes can make a significant difference in how present and effective you feel in each role.

The goal isn't to eliminate the challenge of switching between roles; it's to make these transitions smoother and less draining.[1,2] With intentional practices and self-compassion, we can learn to navigate these daily shifts with more grace and less guilt. After all, our ability to juggle multiple roles isn't a weakness; it's a strength that deserves support and understanding.[2]

The ADHD-Friendly Office: Creating a Workspace That Works for You

I spent years believing my inability to focus while working was just another personal failure. My workspace looked more like an archaeological dig site than an office, with layers of papers, coffee cups, and random supplies creating a timeline of abandoned projects. It wasn't until I discovered how to create an environment that actually worked with my ADHD brain that everything changed.[5]

The breakthrough came one frustrating afternoon when I found myself searching for an important client contract that had mysteriously vanished into what I called the "desktop vortex." After an hour of frantic searching, I found it being used as a coaster for my three-day-old coffee cup. That was my wake-up call; I needed to create a workspace that supported my brain's unique wiring instead of fighting against it.[4]

Let me introduce you to Sophia, a fellow ADHD mom who transformed her chaotic home office into what she calls her "focus sanctuary." Instead of hiding everything in drawers where object permanence issues made them essentially disappear, she installed clear wall organizers and open shelving. "If I can't see it, it doesn't exist in my ADHD brain," she explains. "Now everything has a visible home, and I actually remember what I have and where it is."[4, 6]

Lighting plays a crucial role in maintaining focus, something I learned the hard way after spending months squinting at my laptop in a dim corner. Natural light is ideal, but if that's not possible, full-spectrum lighting that mimics daylight can make a tremendous difference. I positioned my desk to face a window, which not only provides better lighting but also gives my ADHD brain brief micro-breaks when I glance outside.[4]

Jasmine, an accountant working remotely, discovered that her productivity doubled when she created distinct activity zones in her home office. Her main workspace faces a blank wall for focused tasks, while her "project zone" features a large whiteboard for visual planning.[6] "I used to try forcing myself to sit still at my desk all day," she shares. "Now I move between zones based on what my brain needs at the moment, and it's like someone turned up the focus dial."

Sound management was another game-changer for me. After experimenting with different options, I found that my ADHD brain focuses best with a combination of noise-canceling headphones and instrumental music. Tracy, a curriculum developer and mother of two, created what she calls her "focus cocoon" using similar tools. "Even with my kids playing in the next room, I can maintain concentration," she says. "It's like having an invisible force field around my workspace."[4]

One of the most effective changes I made was implementing what I call the "golden triangle, "arranging my most-used items within arm's reach of my chair. This simple adjustment dramatically reduced the number of times I got distracted while getting up to look for something. I keep my planner, favorite pens, and any current project materials within this zone, while less frequently used items live in clearly labeled containers on my open shelving.[4]

Remember, creating an ADHD-friendly office isn't about achieving Instagram-worthy perfection. It's about building a space that works with your brain's natural tendencies rather than against them.[2] Start with one area that causes the most frustration and gradually build from there. Pay attention to what works for you and what doesn't; your ADHD brain will tell you what it needs if you listen to it.

I've learned to schedule weekly "reset" sessions to maintain my systems and prevent overwhelm. Every Friday afternoon, I spend 15 minutes returning items to their homes and adjusting any organizational systems that aren't working.[4] This regular maintenance prevents the kind of build-up that used to send me into complete avoidance of my workspace.

Your ADHD-friendly office will likely look different from mine or anyone else's, and that's exactly as it should be. The goal isn't to copy someone else's perfect system but to create a space that supports your unique way of thinking and working.[2] Trust me, when you find the right combination of elements for your brain, you'll feel the difference in both your productivity and your peace of mind.

Calendar Choreography: Syncing Family and Professional Commitments

I used to think managing my family's calendar was like trying to solve a Rubik's Cube blindfolded; seemingly impossible and guaranteed to end in chaos. The day I found my daughter's dance recital scheduled at the exact same time as my major work presentation, I realized something had to change. Like many ADHD moms, I struggled with the intricate dance of coordinating professional commitments with family obligations.[8]

My friend Roisin's story perfectly captures this challenge. She'd double-booked herself three times in one week: scheduling a client meeting during her son's doctor's appointment, planning to attend two different school events simultaneously, and completely forgetting about a critical work deadline until the night before. "I felt like I was constantly dropping balls," she told me, "until I realized I needed a system that worked with my ADHD brain, not against it."[8]

The breakthrough came when we stopped trying to manage time like our neurotypical counterparts. Traditional calendar systems often assume we can seamlessly transition between tasks and accurately estimate how long activities will take. But for those of us with ADHD, time is more fluid, and transitions require extra buffer zones to account for our unique way of processing schedule changes.[8]

Josephine, an executive assistant and mother of three, transformed her family's scheduling chaos by creating what she calls "time bubbles." Instead of scheduling events back-to-back, she builds in 15-minute buffers between activities. "These bubbles give my ADHD brain time to shift gears," she explains. "Plus, when something inevitably runs long, I'm not throwing off the entire day's schedule."[7]

One of the most effective strategies I've discovered is what I call the "Sunday Sync." Each Sunday evening, I spend twenty minutes aligning my work and family calendars for the week ahead. I look for potential conflicts, identify where I'll need support, and most importantly, build in those essential buffer zones. This weekly check-in helps prevent the last-minute scrambles that used to define my weeks.[7]

Technology can be a powerful ally in this choreography, but only if we use it strategically. I learned this lesson the hard way after trying every calendar app available, only to feel more overwhelmed than ever. Now, I use a single digital calendar with different color codes for work, family, and personal commitments. The visual distinction helps my ADHD brain quickly process different types of obligations without becoming overwhelmed.[7]

Maria, a pediatrician and mother of two, developed what she calls her "calendar triage" system. "I treat schedule conflicts like I treat patients in the ER – assessing urgency and importance before making decisions," she shares. "Some things truly need my presence, while others can be delegated or rescheduled."[8]

The key to successful calendar choreography isn't perfection; it's flexibility and self-compassion. There will still be days when appointments overlap or deadlines sneak up on us. The difference is in how we handle these moments. Instead of spiraling into self-blame, we can view these challenges as opportunities to refine our systems.[7]

Perhaps the most important lesson I've learned is that effective calendar management isn't just about organizing time; it's about honoring our energy levels and attention spans. I now schedule high-stakes work meetings during my peak focus hours and save routine family tasks for times when my attention naturally wanes.[8]

Remember, you're not just managing a calendar: you're orchestrating a complex dance of responsibilities, relationships, and self-care. Permit yourself to experiment until you find the rhythm that works for your unique ADHD brain. After all, the best calendar system isn't the most complex or the most colorful; it's the one you'll actually use."[7, 8]

As we wrap up our exploration of managing the mental load of motherhood with ADHD, let's acknowledge something important: having multiple mental tabs open isn't a weakness; it's simply how our remarkable brains work. Throughout this chapter, we've discovered that success isn't about closing all those tabs; it's about organizing them in a way that makes sense for our unique thinking style.

I'm reminded of Amanda's journey from overwhelm to empowerment. Like many of us, she initially struggled with the constant mental juggling of work deadlines, family schedules, and household responsibilities. Her breakthrough came when she stopped fighting against her browser-like brain and started working with it. By implementing digital tools for capturing racing thoughts and creating designated processing times for different types of tasks, she transformed her mental chaos into manageable energy.

Other stories of revolutionizing work-life balance through intentional time blocking show us that small changes can lead to significant improvements. Success won't be achieved by forcing yourself to think like everyone else; instead, you can build systems that acknowledge and work with your ADHD traits. "Mode switching stations" may help you transition smoothly between work and family responsibilities, reducing the mental strain of constant context switching.

The strategies we've explored aren't about changing how we think; they're about creating systems that work with our natural thinking patterns. Whether it's clear wall organizers that make everything visible for object-permanence challenges, or a focus cocoon that helps you maintain concentration, these solutions succeed because they align with our ADHD brains rather than fight against them.

Before we move forward, I encourage you to choose just one strategy we've discussed to implement this week. Maybe it's setting up a dedicated workspace, creating transition rituals between career and home, or calendar choreography to sync home and work. Remember, you don't need to overhaul your entire life at once. Start small, be patient with yourself, and celebrate the progress you make along the way.

Your mental browser might always have multiple tabs open, but now you have the tools to organize them effectively. Sometimes, those many open tabs lead to the most creative solutions and unexpected connections; another hidden superpower of our ADHD minds. Let's embrace our browser-like brains and use them to create lives that work for us, not against us.

As we close this chapter, remember that juggling career and family isn't about achieving perfect organization; it's about finding harmony between our unique thinking style and the demands of modern motherhood. By understanding and working with our ADHD traits, we can transform what once felt like chaos into a beautiful symphony of organized chaos that actually works.

Chapter 6:

The Digital Mom's Toolbox: Tech Solutions for the ADHD Parent's Brain

Parenting with ADHD in the digital age can feel like both a superpower and a storm. One minute, technology helps you remember picture day, track your child's school schedule, and pay bills with a single tap. The next, you're trapped in ten open tabs, an unfinished grocery order, and a nagging sense you've forgotten something important. The truth is, tech can either fuel the chaos or become your greatest ally, depending on how you use it.

This chapter is your roadmap to making technology work with your ADHD brain, not against it. We'll start by exploring Digital Organization, where you'll learn how to choose apps that fit your thinking style rather than frustrate it. Next comes Smart Home Solutions, showing how automation can take repetitive tasks off your mind and free up mental energy for what matters most. Finally, Digital Boundaries helps you manage your devices without losing focus or joy to constant pings, scrolls, and notifications.

Think of this as your personal digital survival kit: tools designed to support, simplify, and even soothe the ADHD parent's mind. You don't need to master every gadget; you just need the right mix of smart helpers and healthy limits.

Digital Organization: Choosing and Using the Right Apps for Your ADHD Brain

I stared at my phone screen, overwhelmed by the dozen productivity apps I'd downloaded just this week. Each one promised to be the solution to my ADHD struggles, but instead, they'd become yet another source of notification anxiety. The irony wasn't lost on me; I'd downloaded apps to get organized, only to feel more scattered than ever.

If you're like me, you've probably been through the cycle: download an exciting new app, spend hours setting it up perfectly, use it religiously for three days, then completely forget it exists.[2] It's not your fault; our ADHD brains need tools that work with our unique wiring, not against it.

Let me share what happened with Katrina, a mom from my ADHD support group. After missing three important school events despite having them saved in multiple calendar apps, she decided to try something different. She deleted every app except three: one for calendar management, one for task lists, and one for family communication.[3] "The breakthrough came when I stopped trying to fix my brain," she told me, "and started choosing tools that matched how I naturally think."

Katrina spent an hour setting up each app with intention: creating color-coded calendars for different family members, establishing simple categories for tasks, and setting up automation between her apps.[3] When she added an event to her calendar, it automatically created a task list and sent notifications to relevant family members. Within weeks, her digital system was actually working.

The key isn't finding the perfect app; it's finding the right combination that matches your natural tendencies. Think about your typical day and your common pain points. Do you frequently forget appointments? A calendar app with multiple reminders might be your priority.[2] Struggling to keep track of school forms and permission slips? A scanning app that automatically organizes documents could be your solution.

Laura, another mom from our support group, transformed her morning routine with just two carefully chosen apps. She uses her phone's built-in calendar for family scheduling and a simple task manager with voice input for capturing random thoughts.[1] "The game-changer wasn't the apps themselves," she explained, "but learning to trust that I didn't need a complicated system to be a good mom."

When choosing your digital tools, think of them as extensions of your brain rather than replacements for it. The best app is one you'll actually remember to use. Can you set it up in under 15 minutes? Does it take three steps or fewer to add new information? Does it integrate with apps you already use? If not, keep looking.

Remember, you don't need to digitize every aspect of your life overnight. Start with just one area that causes you the most stress.[2] Maybe it's meal planning, or perhaps it's keeping track of school communications. Choose one app that addresses that specific challenge and give yourself time to make it a habit before adding anything else.

Six months after streamlining her digital tools, Laura shared something profound: "My phone isn't just a device anymore; it's become the external hard drive for my ADHD brain, storing everything from school schedules to that brilliant parenting idea I had at 3 AM." Her system wasn't perfect, but it was perfectly suited to her needs.[1, 2]

Your digital organization journey doesn't have to be another source of overwhelm. By choosing tools that work with your natural tendencies and building habits around them gradually, you can create a system that supports rather than stresses you.[1, 2, 3] Remember, the goal isn't to become a different person; it's to find tools that help you be the best version of yourself.

Smart Home Solutions: Automating Routines and Reminders

Standing in my kitchen at 6 AM, staring at the coffeemaker I'd forgotten to set up the night before, I realized something had to change. The morning chaos of missed alarms, forgotten medications, and last-minute lunch packing was taking its toll, not just on me, but on my whole family. Like many ADHD moms, I was drowning in good intentions but struggling with follow-through.[4, 7]

That's when Heidi, a fellow ADHD mom, introduced me to the concept of making my home work smarter, not harder. "My house became my external brain," she told me, describing how she'd transformed her morning chaos into a manageable routine with some strategic automation.[7] "Now, at 7 AM, my lights gradually brighten, my coffee starts brewing automatically, and a gentle reminder plays through my speakers: 'Time for medications.'"

The change in Heidi's household was remarkable. Her children started arriving at the breakfast table without the usual string of reminders, guided by the gentle cues of brightening lights and morning music.[6]

The daily hunt for backpacks and shoes disappeared after she installed motion-activated lights in the mudroom, making it impossible to miss items left out of place.

Holly, another mom from our support group, started even smaller. She began with just a smart speaker in her kitchen, using it to set timers and reminders throughout the day.[6] "I was skeptical at first," she shared, "but having those verbal reminders helped me stay on track without constantly checking my phone." Three months later, she expanded to smart plugs for her kids' bedroom lights, creating a visual bedtime routine that reduced evening battles.

The key is starting with your biggest pain point. For me, it was morning medication management.[6] I invested in a smart outlet for my bedroom lamp and synchronized it with my phone's medication reminder. When it's time for my morning dose, the light pulses gently; a visual cue that's harder to ignore than a phone notification I might easily dismiss.

Amber, a working mom of three, created what she calls her "leaving the house sequence." When she says, "Alexa, we're heading out," it triggers a series of gentle reminders: "Did you pack lunch? Got your homework? Take your medication?" It even checks if the garage door is closed and the stove is off.[6] "It's like having a patient friend who never gets tired of double-checking things," she explains.

But here's the most important lesson I've learned: automation should reduce your mental load, not add to it.[4,7] Start with one pain point; maybe it's morning routines or medication reminders. Give yourself time to adjust before adding more. Daniella, who initially tried to automate everything at once, shared her wisdom: "I overwhelmed myself trying to create the perfect smart home overnight. When I scaled back and focused on just our morning routine, everything clicked."

Think about your daily struggles. Where do you consistently get stuck? Maybe it's remembering to switch the laundry over, or ensuring doors are locked at night.[7] A simple smart plug or automated reminder could be your first step toward a more supportive home environment.

Remember, these tools aren't about replacing your abilities; they're about supporting them.[5, 7] They can't make decisions for you or handle complex situations, but they can take some of the pressure off your working memory and help maintain consistent routines. The goal isn't to create a fully automated home overnight; it's to gradually build a support system that helps manage the mental load of ADHD motherhood.[4, 5, 6, 7]

As Nicola from my support group often says, "My smart home isn't perfect, but it's like having a personal assistant who never gets tired, never judges, and always remembers. For an ADHD mom, that's worth its weight in gold."

Digital Boundaries: Managing Tech Without Getting Overwhelmed

I found myself sitting in the school pickup line, phone in hand, having just spent twenty minutes scrolling through social media instead of reviewing the work presentation I'd planned to edit. Sound familiar? For ADHD moms like us, our smartphones and tablets can feel like both a lifeline and our biggest source of distraction; often simultaneously.[11]

Like Samantha, a mom in my support group who recently confessed, "I picked up my phone to check my daughter's soccer schedule and somehow ended up ordering $200 worth of organizing supplies I probably don't need." We laughed together because we've all been there; our ADHD brains are particularly vulnerable to the endless scroll, the constant notifications, and the allure of digital dopamine hits.[11]

But here's what I've learned: the solution isn't about eliminating technology; it's about creating boundaries that work with our unique brain wiring.[11] Take Sarah, another mom from our group, who transformed her digital overwhelm with what she calls her "traffic light system." She organized her phone's home screen into three zones: green for essential tools like calendar and reminders, yellow for emails and messages that need scheduled check-ins, and red for social media and other potential time-drains.[8, 9]

"The visual organization made all the difference," Sarah explained. "When I'm waiting at pickup, I can instantly see which apps are okay to use without falling down a rabbit hole." Three months after implementing this system, she found herself naturally reaching for her "green" apps first, making better use of those small pockets of time throughout her day.[8, 10]

Fiona, a working mom of three, shared how she reclaimed her evenings with a simple "digital sunset" approach. "At 8 PM, my phone automatically switches to grayscale mode and mutes all non-essential notifications. It's amazing how much less appealing mindless scrolling becomes when everything's in black and white." She now spends her evenings more present with her children, finding that the boundary actually helps her ADHD brain transition to bedtime more easily.[9, 10]

One of the most effective strategies I've discovered is treating our digital attention like a bank account; we need to make intentional withdrawals rather than random impulse purchases.[8] Adele, a single mom with ADHD, started scheduling specific times for email and social media checks, treating them like actual appointments in her calendar. "Instead of constantly responding to every notification, I now batch-process my digital life during designated times. It's not perfect, but it's sustainable."[8, 10]

The key to making these boundaries stick is building them around your natural tendencies rather than fighting against them.[9] If you know you habitually check your phone first thing in the morning, don't try to ban phone use until noon. Instead, create a morning routine that channels that impulse productively; perhaps checking your calendar and daily planning app before allowing yourself to open social media.[8, 9]

Remember, these boundaries aren't about restriction; they're about creating space for what truly matters.[11] Alison, another mom from our group, realized this when her daughter asked, "Mom, do you love your phone more than me?" That question led her to establish phone-free zones in her home, starting with the dinner table. "Now, when my ADHD brain urges me to check my phone during family meals, the physical boundary of having it in another room makes it easier to resist," she shared.[9]

Start small; perhaps with just one boundary that addresses your biggest digital pain point.[9] Maybe it's no phone use during meals, or setting specific times for checking email.[8] Give yourself permission to experiment and adjust until you find what works for your unique situation. Remember, the goal isn't perfect digital discipline; it's about creating sustainable boundaries that help us be more present and productive in our lives.[10]

As Eloise, a mom of twins, recently told me, "I finally realized that every time I set and maintain a digital boundary, I'm not just managing my own overwhelm; I'm modeling healthy technology habits for my children."[9] And sometimes, that's exactly the motivation we need to stick with it, even when our ADHD brains are begging for just one more scroll.[11]

Picture yourself at the end of a long day, your mind still buzzing with unclosed tabs: tomorrow's schedule, that email you need to send, the permission slip buried somewhere on your desk. If you're feeling overwhelmed by the constant mental notifications and browser-like thinking patterns of your ADHD brain, you're not alone. Throughout this chapter, we've explored how our minds work differently, not better or worse, just differently.

We've witnessed how moms have transformed their car-crying moment into a catalyst for change, developing a digital system that helped them manage their mental tabs effectively. A traffic light system for apps can create clear boundaries that work with ADHD brains instead of fighting against them. And stories of streamlining digital tools remind us that sometimes less truly is more when it comes to managing our mental browsers.

Remember, the goal isn't to close all your mental tabs or somehow transform into a single-focus parent. Instead, it's about learning to navigate your browser-brain effectively, choosing which tabs need your attention right now and which can safely run in the background. Whether you're using digital tools to externalize your thoughts, creating smart home systems to reduce your cognitive load, or setting up boundaries to manage digital overwhelm, you're building a support system that works with your natural tendencies rather than against them.

As you move forward, start with just one strategy that resonated with you; maybe it's creating a digital brain dump system or setting up simple smart home automations for a morning routine. Test it, adjust it, and make it your own. Remember that what works for one ADHD mom might not work for another, and that's perfectly okay. The beauty of our ADHD brains is their uniqueness, and the solutions that work best are the ones we adapt to fit our individual needs.

Most importantly, be patient with yourself as you implement these changes. Your mental browser didn't get overloaded overnight, and it won't be reorganized in a day. Celebrate the small victories, like remembering to use your new system or successfully setting and maintaining a digital boundary. Each step forward, no matter how small, is progress toward a more manageable mental load.

In the next chapter, we'll explore the topic of hyperfocus and how to harness this, problem-solve and get the best out of it in daily life. Until then, remember that your ADHD brain isn't broken; it's just running a different operating system, and with the right tools and strategies, you can learn to use its unique features to your advantage.

Chapter 7:

When Mom's Brain Goes Zoom: Using Hyperfocus and Creativity as Superpowers

When an ADHD mom's brain "goes zoom," it can feel both exhilarating and exhausting. One moment, she's laser-focused and creating magic out of chaos; the next, she's wondering where the time went or why the laundry is still in the washer. But within that whirlwind lies something extraordinary: a capacity for deep focus, imaginative leaps, and inventive solutions that often defy convention.

This chapter explores how to turn that rapid-fire mental energy into a powerful tool rather than a source of frustration. We'll look at how hyperfocus, when understood and directed with intention, can fuel creativity and achievement. We'll also uncover how the ADHD brain excels at creative problem-solving, seeing patterns and connections others might miss. Finally, we'll explore ways to build bridges between hyperfocus and daily life, blending passion, productivity, and balance so that the "zoom" moments become sustainable superpowers rather than fleeting bursts.

Harnessing Hyperfocus: Channeling Intense Attention for Maximum Impact

Have you ever looked up from a project to realize hours have vanished like morning mist, leaving behind missed appointments, cold cups of coffee, and that nagging feeling that you've done it again? As an ADHD mom, I've learned that hyperfocus can feel like a superpower and a curse rolled into one fascinating package. It's that state where time becomes meaningless and the world fades away while you're deep in a task that captures your complete attention.[1]

I remember the day I finally understood how to harness this intense focus instead of letting it control me. I was redesigning my daughter's bedroom at 2 AM, completely absorbed in matching color swatches and researching storage solutions, when my phone buzzed with a message from my husband: "Don't forget we have parent-teacher conferences tomorrow morning." That moment sparked a revelation: my hyperfocus wasn't the enemy; I just needed to learn how to direct it purposefully.[1]

The transformation began when I started treating my hyperfocus like a powerful but wild horse that needed gentle guidance rather than harsh control. Instead of fighting against these intense focus periods, I learned to create the right conditions for them to serve me rather than sabotage me. I designated specific times for what I call "deep dive sessions," when my partner knows he's on kid duty, and I can fully immerse myself in tasks that benefit from uninterrupted concentration.[1]

One of my clients, Dee, a marketing executive and mother of three, discovered her own way of working with her hyperfocus. She noticed that her most productive writing sessions happened in the early morning hours, so she started waking up an hour before her family. She created what she calls her "focus nest," a comfortable corner in her home office with noise-canceling headphones, a visual timer within eyesight, and a "do not disturb unless bleeding" sign her kids helped decorate. This dedicated space and time allowed her to channel her hyperfocus into completing important work projects before the day's chaos began.[1]

The key isn't just about finding the right time and space; it's about creating a supportive framework that prevents hyperfocus from derailing the rest of your life. I've learned to set up what I call "focus guardrails," systems that keep me on track without breaking my concentration. This includes setting multiple alarms with gradually increasing urgency, using visual timers that I can't ignore, and having accountability check-ins with my family.[1]

Perhaps the most powerful shift came when I started viewing hyperfocus as a gift rather than a glitch. Those intense periods of concentration can be incredible assets for tackling complex projects, solving creative problems, or diving deep into activities that require sustained attention.[1] The trick is learning to direct this power toward the tasks that truly deserve it, rather than letting it pull you into a three-hour Pinterest session about organizing systems you'll never actually implement.

Remember, working with your hyperfocus rather than against it means accepting that your brain operates differently, and that's okay. It's about building awareness of your triggers, creating environments that support productive focus, and establishing gentle but firm boundaries that help you maintain balance.[1] When managed thoughtfully, hyperfocus can transform from a source of guilt and missed obligations into one of your greatest strengths as an ADHD mom.

Start small: identify one task this week that could benefit from your intense focus, create the conditions for success, and let yourself dive deep without judgment. You might be surprised at how powerful your hyperfocus can be when it's channeled intentionally rather than fighting against it.[1]

The Creative ADHD Brain: Problem-Solving Outside the Box

Like many ADHD moms, I used to think my scattered thinking was a liability until the day I found myself creating an elaborate treasure hunt to help my daughter remember her multiplication tables. That's when I realized my "different" way of approaching problems wasn't a flaw; it was actually a superpower in disguise.

Our ADHD brains don't follow the usual straight path from A to B. Instead, we bounce around like a pinball, lighting up different connections and possibilities along the way. While this can sometimes feel chaotic, it's precisely this unique wiring that allows us to see solutions others might miss.[1]

Take Monica, a mother of three who transformed her family's morning struggles into an innovative game. After months of battling with traditional checklists and routines, she noticed how engaged her kids became when playing video games. Instead of fighting their resistance, she created "Morning Mission," complete with achievement levels, power-ups for completing tasks early, and special bonus rounds for helping siblings. What started as a desperate attempt to get everyone out the door became a creative solution that other parents in her ADHD support group began adopting for their own families.[1]

Our ability to see possibilities where others see problems is one of our greatest strengths.[1] Olivia, who works from home, struggled with constant interruptions during important calls until she created the "Ninja Mission Center." During calls, her kids became secret agents with special silent missions, complete with hand signals and reward points for maintaining stealth operations. What could have been an ongoing source of stress became an opportunity for creative engagement that actually worked.

Charlotte's approach to homework battles with her daughter shows how our outside-the-box thinking can transform daily challenges.[1] Rather than forcing her daughter to sit at a desk (which wasn't working for either of them), she created mobile learning stations throughout the house. Math problems could be solved while bouncing on an exercise ball, vocabulary words were practiced during kitchen dance parties, and reading comprehension happened in a cozy tent fort. Not only did her daughter's grades improve, but their evening routine transformed from a source of tension to a time of creative connection.

The beauty of our ADHD creativity lies in its flexibility and adaptability.[1] When Claire couldn't keep track of her children's chores using traditional charts, she created a family "quest board" with movable task cards and weekly "boss challenges." Her children not only completed their chores more consistently but also began creating their own quests and rewards.

I've learned to embrace those moments when my mind wanders into unexpected territory.[2] Some of my best parenting solutions have come from making connections that might seem strange to others but make perfect sense to my ADHD brain. Like the time I turned our laundry sorting into a "color rescue mission" after noticing how my son loved organizing his Lego blocks by color.

Your ADHD brain's tendency to think differently isn't a bug; it's a feature that can lead to innovative solutions for everyday challenges.[2] When you find yourself thinking "too far outside the box," remember that's exactly where some of the best ideas live. After all, who needs a box when you can build a rocket ship instead?

The key is learning to trust your unique perspective and permitting yourself to experiment with unconventional solutions.[2] Keep track of your creative wins; they'll remind you that your different way of thinking isn't just valid, it's valuable. Your ADHD brain's creative potential is like a Swiss Army knife; it has multiple tools that can be applied in countless ways to solve the daily puzzles of parenting.

So the next time you come up with a solution that seems too wild or unconventional, remember: that's your superpower at work.[1] And in a world that often demands creative solutions to complex challenges, your ADHD brain might just be exactly what's needed.

Building Bridges Between Hyperfocus and Daily Life: Creating Sustainable Systems

Think of your ADHD brain as a powerful but unpredictable engine; sometimes running at full throttle, other times idling unexpectedly.[3] As a mom with ADHD, I've learned that the key isn't trying to maintain a constant speed, but rather creating systems that work with these natural fluctuations.

I remember the day this clicked for me. I was deep in "organization mode," completely revamping our family's command center at 2 AM while a sink full of dishes waited and tomorrow's lunches remained unpacked. My hyperfocus had struck again,[3] and while the color-coded calendar system I created was impressive, it wasn't helping with the immediate needs of daily life.

That's when I realized I needed to build bridges between these intense periods of hyperfocus and the steady flow of daily responsibilities.[3, 4, 5] The solution wasn't fighting against my brain's natural tendencies, but rather creating systems that could capture and channel that energy productively.

Take Gemma, one of the moms in my support group, who transformed her hyperfocus tendencies into a superpower.[3] Instead of letting herself get swept away in hours-long organizing sprees, she created what she calls her "Focus Funnel" system. When hyperfocus hits, she quickly captures her ideas in a designated notebook, then channels that energy into 25-minute sprints using a timer. This way, she can harness her intense focus while maintaining awareness of other responsibilities.[3, 4]

The key to building sustainable systems lies in understanding that our ADHD brains work differently.[3, 6] Rather than trying to maintain constant attention across all tasks, we can create what I call "momentum moments," strategic points throughout the day where we leverage our natural energy surges.

Una, another mom I work with, discovered this when she stopped fighting her tendency to hyperfocus during late evening hours.[4, 5] Instead of feeling guilty about her "weird" timing, she reorganized her schedule to tackle detail-oriented tasks after her kids' bedtime. She created a simple system she calls her "Night Owl Power Hour," complete with a dedicated workspace and clear boundaries about when to stop.

One of the most powerful bridges you can build is what I call the "Reality Anchor," a simple but effective system that keeps you connected to daily needs even during intense focus periods.[5, 6] This might look like setting multiple alarms with specific task reminders, using visual cues in your workspace, or establishing regular check-in points throughout the day.

Isla, a working mom of three, created her version using what she calls "Focus Flags," colored Post-it notes that she can quickly jot down urgent tasks on without breaking her concentration.[5] These visual reminders help her transition between deep work and daily responsibilities without losing momentum.

Remember, the goal isn't to eliminate hyperfocus; it's one of our superpowers, after all.[3] Instead, we're creating flexible systems that help us harness its energy while maintaining the flow of daily life.

Think of it like installing shock absorbers on a powerful car; they don't reduce the engine's power, they just make the ride smoother.

Start small when building your bridges.[4, 5] Choose one area where hyperfocus tends to create challenges and experiment with a simple system to manage it. Maybe it's setting up automated reminders for transition times or designating specific spaces for deep work versus quick tasks. The key is finding what works for your unique brain and lifestyle.

Through trial and error, you'll discover your own rhythm of balancing intense focus periods with daily responsibilities.[4, 5] The beauty of creating these bridges is that they don't just make life more manageable; they allow us to fully embrace and utilize our ADHD traits while keeping our family life running smoothly.

As we wrap up our exploration of hyperfocus and how to harness and channel it, let's acknowledge a fundamental truth: our ADHD brains don't fit neatly into traditional organizational boxes, and that's perfectly okay. Throughout this chapter, we've discovered that lasting routines aren't built on rigid rules or elaborate systems, but on understanding and working with our unique neural wiring.

Beth's journey from overwhelming charts to sustainable habits reminds us that success often comes through small, intentional changes. Her transformation didn't happen overnight; it began with a single, manageable step: placing medication by her bedside. This seemingly tiny action became the foundation for a morning routine that actually worked, proving that progress isn't about perfection but about finding what truly fits our ADHD brains.

Remember the approach of creating a "traffic light system" for managing energy levels? This creative approach demonstrates how our ADHD minds can turn challenges into innovations. By working with her natural rhythms instead of against them, she didn't just build a routine; she created a whole new way of communicating with her family about energy and capacity.

Maria's experience with her "focus funnel" system showed us how hyperfocus, often seen as a challenge, can become a powerful ally in establishing routines. By channeling her intense focus periods into productive sprints, she transformed what could have been a liability into a strength. Her approach reminds us that our ADHD traits aren't flaws to fix but potential advantages to harness.

As you move forward with creating your own routines, remember that sustainability comes from alignment with your natural tendencies, not from fighting against them. Start with something small that feels genuinely manageable: maybe it's placing your keys in a consistent spot, setting up a simple morning playlist, or creating a visual reminder for medication. Whatever you choose, make it something that works with your brain rather than against it.

The most powerful routines often grow from these modest beginnings. A weekly meal prep system may not start as a comprehensive plan; it may begin with simply keeping favorite breakfast ingredients in an easily visible spot. But, months later, the entire family may benefit from a flexible but reliable meal planning routine that accommodates their changing needs and energy levels.

Remember, creating routines that stick isn't about becoming a different person or forcing yourself into someone else's system. It's about building frameworks that honor your unique brain while supporting your daily life. Some days will flow smoothly, others might feel more chaotic, and both are perfectly normal parts of the journey.

As you experiment with different approaches, keep these words in mind: "I stopped trying to be perfectly organized and started being perfectly me instead." This perspective captures the heart of what we've explored in this chapter: that sustainable routines grow from self-acceptance and understanding, not from rigid adherence to traditional expectations.

Take a moment now to consider one small change you could implement tomorrow. Something that feels both doable and meaningful. That's where lasting change begins; not in grand overhauls or complex systems, but in simple, intentional steps that align with your natural way of thinking and being. Your path to creating sustainable routines won't look like anyone else's, and that's exactly as it should be.

Chapter 8:

The 'Me Time' Mission: Self-Care Strategies for the Overwhelmed ADHD Mom

There's a familiar chaos that hums through the life of an ADHD mom: the endless lists, the misplaced keys, the half-drunk coffee, and the feeling that there's never enough time or energy to simply breathe. Between the demands of caring for others and the constant mental noise that ADHD can bring, self-care often slips to the bottom of the list. Yet it's precisely in these hectic, overstimulating moments that caring for yourself becomes essential, not optional.

This chapter is your permission slip to slow down, even briefly, and to redefine what "self-care" really means in your life. You'll learn how to discover micro-moments of calm, where peace can exist even in a five-minute window. You'll explore how energy management, not rigid schedules, can help you work with your natural rhythms instead of against them. And most importantly, you'll practice building boundaries that protect your wellbeing, replacing guilt with empowerment.

Think of this chapter as your personal mission map: practical, compassionate, and designed for real life; the kind that spills milk, misplaces planners, and still shows up every day with love and determination.

Micro-Moments of Self-Care: Finding Peace in Five-Minute Intervals

Lily stood in her kitchen, mechanically stirring her third cup of cold coffee while responding to work emails on her phone and half-listening to her children argue over breakfast. She couldn't remember the last time she'd actually sat down to enjoy a hot cup of coffee from start to finish. The thought made her chest tighten with a familiar mix of frustration and guilt; another simple thing she couldn't seem to manage.

As ADHD moms, we're often the last ones on our own priority lists. Traditional self-care advice feels like just another set of impossible standards we're failing to meet.[1] An hour-long morning meditation? Twenty minutes of journaling? These suggestions can feel almost laughable when we're struggling to remember if we've brushed our teeth today.

But what if we could reimagine self-care in a way that actually works for our ADHD brains? That's what Flo discovered one hectic Tuesday morning. While hiding in her pantry eating chocolate chips straight from the bag (we've all been there), she had an epiphany: maybe she needed to think smaller. Instead of trying to carve out huge chunks of time that never materialized, she could create tiny moments of peace within her existing routine.

Flo started simple. She began taking three deep breaths while waiting for her coffee to brew each morning. Then she added a favorite scented lotion to her car's console, applying it mindfully at red lights. Soon, she found herself discovering more opportunities for these micro-moments throughout her day: playing her favorite song during school drop-off, stretching for 30 seconds while supervising tooth-brushing time, and even taking actual breaks during her designated "bathroom breaks."

The key was attaching these moments to things she was already doing rather than trying to create entirely new routines.[1] Rosie, another mom from our ADHD support group, keeps a gratitude journal by her coffee maker. While the coffee brews, she writes down just one thing she's grateful for. No pressure for lengthy entries or perfect handwriting; just one thought, one moment of mindfulness, tied to something she does every day anyway.

What makes these micro-moments particularly effective for ADHD brains is their flexibility.[1] There's no failing, no falling behind, no complex system to maintain. Some days you might hit all your planned pause points, other days maybe just one or two. Each moment of self-care stands alone, valuable in itself, without the pressure of perfect consistency.

Isabella, a working mom of three, created what she calls her "Reset Kit," a collection of quick tools she can access whenever she needs a moment of peace.[3] She keeps a tiny bottle of lavender oil in her desk drawer, a playlist of three-minute mood-lifting songs on her phone, and a smooth worry stone in her pocket. These small touches help her find moments of calm, even on the most chaotic days.

The most powerful shift happens when we start viewing these micro-moments not as indulgences but as essential maintenance for our ADHD brains.[1, 2] Just as we wouldn't expect our phones to run without charging, we can't sustain our energy without these small recharging moments throughout the day.

Sometimes self-care looks like ordering pizza instead of cooking so you can have fifteen minutes to decompress. Sometimes it's saying no to the PTA meeting because you know it will deplete your limited energy reserves. And yes, sometimes it's eating chocolate chips in the pantry; but now we can do it mindfully, without guilt, knowing it's part of taking care of ourselves in a way that actually works for our unique brains.[1,2]

Remember, you don't need to transform your entire life overnight. Start with just one micro-moment today.[1] Maybe it's three deep breaths while waiting for your coffee, or a minute of stretching while supervising homework time. These tiny acts of self-care might seem insignificant, but they add up to create a sustainable pattern of self-nurturing that actually fits into real life with ADHD.[1,4]

Energy Management vs. Time Management: Understanding Your Personal Battery

Ella stared at her to-do list, carefully organized by time slots, and felt that familiar knot of anxiety tightening in her chest. Despite meticulously planning every hour, she still felt exhausted by 2 PM, barely able to focus on her afternoon meetings. The pristine schedule mocked her inability to stick to it, adding another layer of guilt to her already overwhelmed mind.[4]

As ADHD moms, we're often told that better time management is the answer to our struggles. We've tried every productivity system, downloaded countless planning apps, and created elaborate schedules that look perfect on paper. But here's what nobody tells us: for ADHD brains, managing energy is far more crucial than managing time.[1, 4]

Take Phoebe's story. She used to schedule her most challenging work tasks for late afternoon because that's when her calendar had the most free time. But she consistently found herself unable to focus, often spending hours staring at her computer screen while her anxiety mounted. Everything changed when she started paying attention to her energy patterns instead of just the clock.[1]

"I realized I had been fighting against my natural rhythms," Phoebe shared. "My brain is sharpest in the morning, right after my medication kicks in. Now I schedule my most demanding tasks then, even if it means shifting my entire day around."[1, 4]

Understanding your personal battery isn't just about recognizing when you're most productive; it's about acknowledging that your energy fluctuates throughout the day in a unique pattern. Some of us are morning powerhouses but crash after lunch. Others take hours to warm up but hit their stride in the afternoon. Neither pattern is wrong; they're just different operating systems.[1]

Harper, another mom from our ADHD support group, discovered that her energy crashes weren't just about time management; they were about task transitions. "I used to try to switch from creative work to administrative tasks multiple times a day because that's what the time-blocking experts recommended. But each transition drained my battery faster than I could recharge it."[4]

Now Harper batches similar tasks together, allowing her brain to stay in one mode longer. She handles all her emails and paperwork during her afternoon energy dip when her creative energy is naturally lower anyway. This simple shift has transformed her productivity and, more importantly, her sense of accomplishment.[3, 4]

The key to managing your personal battery lies in becoming a curious observer of your own patterns. Start noticing when you naturally feel most focused, when you tend to get overwhelmed, and what activities drain or energize you. Keep a simple energy log for a week; just jot down how you're feeling at different points in the day.[1, 4]

Millie found that short breaks between tasks weren't enough to recharge her battery; she needed what she calls "energy pivots." "If I've been doing focused work, I might take a 10-minute break to dance with my kids or step outside. The physical movement and change of environment recharge me faster than sitting scrolling on my phone."[1]

Remember, energy management isn't about pushing through when you're depleted; it's about working with your natural rhythms. Sometimes the most productive thing you can do is rest, even if your schedule says otherwise. This might mean taking a power nap during your lunch break or going for a quick walk between meetings.[1]

The truth is, traditional time management systems weren't designed for ADHD brains. They assume a steady, predictable energy flow that most of us simply don't have. By shifting our focus from managing minutes to managing energy, we can create sustainable systems that work with our unique wiring instead of against it.[1, 4]

Start small; pick one task tomorrow and try scheduling it based on your energy level rather than just your available time. Notice how different it feels to work with your natural rhythms instead of fighting against them. Remember, you're not failing at time management; you're just ready for a different approach that honors how your brain actually works.[1, 4]

Building Boundaries: Learning to Say No Without Guilt

Matilda stared at her phone, her heart racing as she read the text from the PTA president asking her to coordinate the spring fundraiser. Her fingers instinctively started typing "Sure, I'd love to..." before she caught herself, remembering how overwhelmed she'd felt last month when she'd taken on three different volunteer commitments while barely managing her own household tasks.

As ADHD moms, saying no often feels impossible. Our impulsivity drives us to say yes before we can properly assess our capacity, while our heightened emotional sensitivity makes us particularly vulnerable to the guilt that follows when we do set boundaries.[2, 4] We worry that saying no will disappoint others or confirm their worst suspicions about our reliability.

Take Ruby's story: "I used to say yes to everything because I thought it would prove I was capable despite my ADHD. I was drowning in commitments until my therapist helped me realize that saying yes to everything was actually making me less reliable for the things that truly mattered."

The turning point for Ruby came when she learned to pause before responding to requests. She developed what she calls her "boundary pause," a simple but powerful practice of saying, "Let me check my calendar and get back to you," before making any commitments.[3] This small buffer gives her ADHD brain time to move past the initial impulse and thoughtfully consider whether she truly has the capacity to take on more.

Maisie, another mom from our support group, found success with what she calls her "energy budget." She visualizes her daily energy like a bank account, with different activities requiring different amounts of withdrawal.[3, 4] Before saying yes to anything new, she considers her current balance and outstanding commitments. "It helps me recognize that saying no isn't about being mean or unhelpful; it's about being responsible with my limited energy resources."

One of the most powerful tools for building boundaries is having ready responses that feel both kind and firm. Instead of apologizing or making excuses, try simple statements like, "That sounds wonderful, but I need to pass this time," or "I wish I could help, but my plate is full right now."[3] Notice how these responses don't include the word "sorry," because protecting your energy isn't something that requires an apology.

Eliza, who struggled with chronic overcommitment, found freedom in being honest about her ADHD when appropriate. "Sometimes I simply say, 'I know myself well enough to know that wouldn't be a good fit for how my brain works.' It's liberating to acknowledge my needs without shame."

The beautiful irony about boundary setting is that when we get better at saying no, we become more reliable with our yeses.[2] Violet discovered this after starting what she calls her "Not Now" list. Whenever she says no to something, she adds it to the list with a quick note about why it wasn't right for her at that time. After a few months, she realized that saying no to those things had allowed her to be more present and effective in the commitments that truly mattered to her family.

Start small; practice saying no to low-stakes requests first.[3] Use digital tools to track your commitments and prevent overextending. Build in pause points before adding anything new to your schedule. Remember, boundaries aren't walls that keep people out; they're filters that help you preserve your energy for what matters most.

As Esme, a mom of three with ADHD, puts it: "Setting boundaries isn't just about saying no to others; it's about saying yes to yourself. Every time I protect my energy and attention, I'm actually being a better mom, because I'm showing up fully for the things I do commit to."

Your time, energy, and attention are precious resources that deserve to be protected.[2] Each boundary you set is an act of self-respect and a gift to your family, allowing you to show up as the mother you want to be for the moments that truly matter.

Standing in her kitchen surrounded by abandoned organizational systems, sticky notes, half-filled planners, and three different calendar apps on her phone, Thea finally understood that creating sustainable routines wasn't about forcing herself into someone else's perfect system. It was about building flexible frameworks that worked with her ADHD brain, not against it.

As we've explored throughout this chapter, 'me' time is important, and self-care is crucial. You need to build in micro moments, manage your energy and set boundaries. The key to creating routines that actually stick isn't perfection; it's progress. Like Freya, who transformed her chaotic mornings by focusing on just three anchor points instead of an elaborate schedule, you've learned that sometimes less structure creates more stability. Her success didn't come from forcing herself to follow a rigid timeline, but from understanding how her ADHD brain worked and building flexibility into her system.

We've discovered that energy management matters more than time management for our ADHD brains. Remember Harper's story of trying to schedule demanding tasks during her afternoon energy dip? By shifting her most challenging work to match her natural energy peaks, she found a sustainable rhythm that actually worked. Your energy patterns might look different, and that's exactly as it should be.

The section on boundary-setting reminded us that protecting our energy isn't selfish; it's essential. Ruby's journey showed us how learning to pause before saying yes didn't just reduce her overwhelm; it made her more reliable for the commitments she did choose to make. Those micro-moments of self-care we discussed aren't luxuries; they're necessary maintenance for our unique brains.

As you move forward, remember that building routines that stick isn't about becoming a different person: it's about creating systems that work for the wonderful, creative, spontaneous person you already are. Your ADHD brain might not fit into conventional routine-building advice, but that doesn't mean you can't create structure in your life. It just means you get to do it your way.

Think about the small changes you've identified while reading this chapter. Maybe you've recognized your peak energy hours, or perhaps you're just beginning to understand why previous routines haven't worked for you. Each of these insights is valuable, moving you closer to a system that truly supports your life.

In the next chapter, we'll look at family team building and teaching kids to thrive with your ADHD leadership. But for now, take a moment to acknowledge how far you've come. Remember, the most sustainable routine is the one you can actually maintain, even if it looks nothing like what works for anyone else. Keep experimenting, stay flexible, and most importantly, be patient with yourself as you find your own path to creating routines that actually stick; and remember to build in essential 'me' time with micro-moments, energy management and boundaries.

Chapter 9:

Family Team Building: Teaching Kids to Thrive with Your ADHD Leadership

Parenting with ADHD isn't about striving for conventional perfection; it's about rewriting the playbook so your family can thrive as a dynamic, adaptable team. When you lead with empathy, creativity, and authenticity, your ADHD becomes more than a label; it becomes a leadership model your children can learn from. Your energy, spontaneity, and problem-solving instincts can inspire your kids to see differences not as limitations, but as strengths that power your family's unique rhythm.

This chapter explores how to create a home where every member's brain works differently—and that's something to celebrate. You'll learn how to build a neurodiversity-affirming environment that honours different thinking styles, discover collaborative systems that genuinely stick (even when executive function gets tricky), and foster resilience in your children so they can navigate life's challenges with confidence and heart.

When families operate as teams, with everyone's strengths in play and everyone's voice valued, ADHD leadership becomes a shared journey of growth, not a balancing act. Together, you'll move from surviving household chaos to building a thriving ecosystem of understanding, flexibility, and joy.

Creating a Neurodiversity-Affirming Home Environment: Celebrating Different Thinking Styles

Margot stared at the scattered papers on her kitchen counter; another failed attempt at creating the "perfect" organizational system she'd seen on Pinterest. Her ADHD brain rebelled against the rigid categories and complex color-coding, while her daughter's artwork remained stuffed in random drawers instead of being celebrated on the walls. In that moment of frustration, she realized she'd been trying to force her neurodivergent family into a neurotypical box.

Many of us know this struggle intimately; the constant pressure to conform to traditional organizing methods and parenting approaches that simply don't align with how our brains work. We've all had those moments where we've felt like we're somehow failing our families because we can't maintain the picture-perfect systems that seem to work so effortlessly for others.[1]

But here's the truth I've learned through years of working with ADHD families: our different thinking styles aren't deficits to be corrected; they're unique strengths to be celebrated. Take Erin, one of the moms in my support group, who transformed her home environment after embracing this mindset. Instead of fighting against her family's tendency to be visual thinkers, she created a giant wall calendar with removable sticky notes for appointments and tasks.[2,3] Her children, who previously resisted traditional planning methods, eagerly participated in moving the colorful notes around and adding their own reminders.

The key to creating a truly neurodiversity-affirming home isn't about implementing perfect systems; it's about understanding and working with each family member's unique brain wiring. When Liz's son struggled with conventional homework routines, she noticed he thought best while moving. Instead of forcing him to sit still at a desk, she created a "homework path" in their backyard where he could walk while working through math problems. His grades improved, but more importantly, his confidence soared because his natural learning style was honored rather than suppressed.[2]

One of the most powerful changes we can make is shifting our language around differences. In my own home, we've replaced phrases like "paying attention" with "focusing your energy," and "getting distracted" with "noticing different things." This simple shift helps everyone recognize that there's no single "right" way to think or learn.

Creating a neurodiversity-affirming environment also means celebrating unconventional solutions. When Scarlett's daughter struggled with morning routines, they worked together to create a "getting ready dance party" where each task had its own song.[3] What might seem chaotic to others became a joyful, effective routine that worked with her daughter's need for movement and stimulation.

Remember, our children are watching how we treat ourselves. When we embrace our own neurodivergent traits with compassion and creativity, we show them that their unique thinking styles are valuable too.[1] This might mean openly discussing our own challenges and solutions, like explaining why we use noise-canceling headphones during focused work or how we break big tasks into smaller, manageable pieces.

The beauty of a neurodiversity-affirming home is that it creates space for everyone to thrive in their own way. Nancy, another mom from my support group, transformed her family's evening routine by recognizing that her children needed different types of wind-down activities. While her older son benefited from quiet reading time, her younger daughter needed sensory activities to regulate her energy.[2] Instead of forcing them into the same bedtime routine, she created separate spaces that honored their individual needs.

Remember, creating a neurodiversity-affirming home is a journey, not a destination. It's about progress, not perfection. Start small; perhaps by designating a calm-down corner with fidget toys and comfort items, or by introducing family meetings where everyone's voice and ideas are equally valued. The goal isn't to create a perfect environment, but rather a home where different thinking styles are understood, respected, and celebrated.[2, 4]

Family Systems That Stick: Collaborative Problem-Solving Techniques

Zara stood in her kitchen, surrounded by half-finished chore charts and abandoned routine plans, fighting back tears of frustration. Her latest attempt at creating a family organization system had lasted exactly three days before falling apart. Like many ADHD moms, she'd tried countless approaches she'd found online, but traditional family management strategies just didn't seem to stick for her neurodivergent household.[5]

What Zara discovered through her journey, and what I've learned through working with countless ADHD families, is that lasting family systems aren't about imposing perfect routines. They're about creating collaborative solutions that work with, not against, your family's unique dynamics.[5, 6]

Take Iris, a mom from my support group, who transformed her family's morning chaos by involving her children in designing their routine. Instead of presenting a pre-made schedule, she sat down with her kids and asked, "What would make our mornings easier?" To her surprise, her eight-year-old suggested setting out clothes the night before, while her teenager proposed a shared family calendar app. By giving everyone a voice in the solution, she created buy-in that traditional top-down approaches had never achieved.[5]

Collaborative problem-solving works because it honors everyone's perspective and needs.[5] When Bella's family struggled with maintaining their household chores, she turned it into a family brainstorming session. Together, they identified pain points and proposed solutions. Her son, who struggled with traditional chore charts, created a game-like system where family members earned points for completed tasks. Her daughter, who often felt overwhelmed by big tasks, suggested breaking down cleaning jobs into smaller, more manageable steps.[5, 7]

The key to making these systems stick lies in flexibility and ongoing communication. Regular family meetings become less about enforcing rules and more about checking in: What's working? What isn't? How can we adjust? Molly, another mom in my group, schedules weekly "family team huddles" over Sunday breakfast. These casual conversations help catch small issues before they become big problems and allow the family to celebrate their successes together.[5]

Remember, collaborative problem-solving isn't just about creating systems; it's about building trust and understanding within your family.[5] When Lyla's teenage daughter repeatedly missed her curfew, instead of immediately imposing consequences, she opened a dialogue. They discovered her daughter was struggling with time blindness, a common ADHD trait. Together, they brainstormed solutions, eventually settling on using location-sharing apps and setting phone alarms as gentle reminders.[5, 6]

One of the most powerful aspects of this approach is how it transforms "problem behaviors" into opportunities for growth and connection.[5] When Tom, age 10, consistently forgot to pack his school bag, his mom, Gracie, resisted the urge to simply pack it for him. Instead, they worked together to create a visual checklist with photographs of each item needed. Not only did this solve the immediate problem, but it also taught Tom valuable organizational skills while preserving his sense of autonomy.[5, 7]

The beauty of collaborative problem-solving is that it grows with your family. As children develop new capabilities and face new challenges, the systems can evolve.[5] Karen's family reviews and updates their shared agreements quarterly, allowing everyone to contribute fresh ideas and adjust responsibilities as needed. This flexibility helps prevent the rigid routines that often fail in ADHD households.[5, 6]

Start small when implementing collaborative problem-solving in your home. Choose one specific challenge, perhaps morning routines or homework time, and gather your family for a brainstorming session. Make it fun: use colorful markers, serve snacks, and celebrate every suggestion, no matter how unusual. Remember, sometimes the most effective solutions come from unexpected places.[5]

As you build these collaborative systems, you'll likely notice something remarkable: your role shifts from enforcer to facilitator.[5] You're no longer solely responsible for making everything work; instead, you're guiding your family in creating solutions together. This not only lightens your mental load but also helps your children develop valuable problem-solving skills they'll carry into adulthood.[5, 6, 7]

Building Resilience Together: Teaching Kids to Navigate Challenges with Confidence

I found my daughter sobbing in her room after another tough day at school. Her ADHD brain, so much like my own, had struggled to keep up with the rapid-fire instructions in math class. As I held her, I realized that this moment wasn't just about homework; it was an opportunity to teach her the resilience that had taken me decades to learn.[1, 4]

As ADHD moms, we often feel an extra weight of responsibility when it comes to helping our children navigate life's challenges. We've walked this path ourselves, stumbling through the same obstacles of organization, focus, and self-doubt.[1, 4] But what if I told you that our experiences, including our struggles, could become our greatest teaching tools?[1, 8]

Take Summer's story: Her son Alex was ready to quit the school band after forgetting his instrument three times in two weeks. Instead of jumping in with a solution, Summer shared her own story about how she'd learned to cope with similar challenges at work. Together, they brainstormed ideas, eventually creating a visual reminder system by the front door.[2, 8] More importantly, Alex learned that setbacks weren't failures; they were opportunities to problem-solve.[1]

Building resilience isn't about avoiding mistakes or preventing challenges; it's about developing the confidence to face them head-on.[8, 4] When Eden's daughter was overwhelmed by a big project, Eden broke down her own work presentation process, showing how she tackled large tasks in smaller chunks.[2, 8] "Sometimes my ADHD brain feels like it's climbing a mountain," she explained, "but we can handle any mountain if we take it one step at a time."

Emotional regulation plays a crucial role in building resilience.[4] In our house, we've created what we call our "feeling station," a quiet corner with fidget toys, breathing cards, and comfort items. When my son feels frustrated with homework, he knows he can take a break there to reset. This simple tool has helped him learn to recognize and manage his emotions before they become overwhelming.[4]

Elodie, another mom from my support group, transformed her family's approach to challenges by introducing what she calls "growth story time." Each evening at dinner, family members share something that went wrong and how they handled it.[1, 4] Her children began to see challenges as normal parts of life rather than personal failures. More importantly, they learned that everyone, even parents, faces obstacles and finds ways to overcome them.[1]

One of the most powerful ways we can build resilience is by modeling self-compassion.[14, 4] When I forgot about the school bake sale (again), instead of berating myself, I walked my children through my recovery process: "Okay, we forgot the bake sale. That happens sometimes with

ADHD brains. Let's think about what we can do now." This simple shift from shame to problem-solving helps our children develop a healthier response to their own mistakes.[1]

Remember that building resilience is a journey, not a destination.[8, 4] Some days will be harder than others, and that's okay. The goal isn't to eliminate challenges but to help our children develop the confidence and tools to face them. By sharing our own experiences, celebrating effort over perfection, and maintaining a growth mindset, we can help our children develop the resilience they need to thrive.[1, 4]

As Rachel, whose teenage daughter recently started college, told me: "The biggest gift we can give our kids isn't protection from challenges - it's the confidence to know they can handle them."[8] Her daughter now uses the same resilience-building strategies they practiced at home to manage her university workload, proving that these skills last well beyond childhood.

Through our own journey with ADHD, we've learned valuable lessons about adapting, persevering, and growing through challenges.[1, 8] By sharing these lessons with our children, not from a place of perfect expertise, but from one of understanding and experience, we help them build the resilience they'll need for their own unique paths.[1, 8, 4]

Picture this: it's 9 PM, and you're still at your desk, trying to finish a presentation while mentally calculating if you remembered to sign your child's permission slip for tomorrow. Your phone buzzes with a work email just as you realize you forgot to defrost dinner for tomorrow night. Sound familiar? This is the daily juggling act of the working ADHD mom; a unique blend of professional ambition and parental responsibility, all filtered through our beautifully complex ADHD brains.

As we've explored throughout this chapter, success isn't about achieving some mythical perfect balance or completely transforming how your brain works. It's about creating systems and strategies that work with your unique wiring while honoring both your career aspirations and your role as a mother.

We've seen how workplace challenges can be transformed into opportunities by embracing ADHD traits rather than fighting them. Having ADHD gives us a tendency to think outside the box, our ability to hyperfocus when engaged, and our natural creativity can become professional assets when properly channeled.

It is possible to journey from chaos to confidence. Success isn't about becoming a different person; it's about working with our natural tendencies. By creating clear transitions between work and home modes, setting up an ADHD-friendly workspace, and building strong support systems both at work and home, we can find our own rhythm.

Perhaps the most powerful lesson we've uncovered is that being a working mom with ADHD isn't about choosing between career success and present parenting. Instead, it's about finding innovative ways to integrate both roles while honoring your neurodivergent needs. Whether that means using technology to manage competing demands, creating visual systems for task management, or building support networks that understand your unique challenges, the key is finding solutions that feel authentic to you.

As you move forward from this chapter, remember that your journey doesn't have to look like anyone else's. Your ADHD brain might take a different path to success, and that's not just okay; it's valuable. Those moments when you find creative solutions to workplace challenges or help your team see problems from a new perspective? That's your ADHD brain showing up as a superpower.

In our next chapter, we'll explore how important it is to build your village and create a support system of people who understand ADHD motherhood. But for now, take a moment to appreciate how far you've come. You're not just surviving as a working mom with ADHD; you're showing your children what it means to embrace who you are while pursuing your goals, and you're leading your family in the best way possible by creating a neurodiverse-affirming home, collaborating and problem-solving together and building resilience.

Remember, every system you create, every boundary you set, and every time you choose to work with your ADHD instead of against it, you're building a stronger foundation for both your career and your family life. You've got this, mama, and you're not alone on this journey.

Chapter 10:

Building Your Village: Creating Support Systems That Understand ADHD Motherhood

Motherhood can already feel like juggling flaming torches, but for moms with ADHD, it often feels like juggling those torches while riding a unicycle, on an uphill road. Between managing households, emotional overwhelm, and constant mental noise, the need for a supportive network isn't just important; it's essential. Yet many ADHD mothers find themselves isolated, misunderstood, or judged for the way their brains operate and their energy fluctuates.

This chapter explores how to move from that lonely space into community. It begins with finding your tribe; those who "get it," who understand why some days feel like chaos and others surge with unstoppable creativity. You'll learn where to meet other ADHD parents who share your rhythms and relief at being seen.

Next, we'll look at how to communicate your specific ADHD needs to family and friends in ways that build empathy instead of defensiveness. Explaining how your brain works can open the door to honest, supportive conversations rather than friction.

Finally, we'll focus on creating balanced, reciprocal support systems. Because genuine connection isn't only about receiving help; it's about offering it too, in rhythms that honour your energy, boundaries, and capacity.

Together, these pages will help you build a village: not a perfect one, but one rooted in understanding, respect, and shared humanity. It's time to stop doing ADHD motherhood alone.

Finding Your Tribe: Connecting with Other ADHD Parents

Eleanor sat in her parked car outside the local coffee shop, her heart racing as she contemplated walking into her first ADHD moms' support group meeting. After years of nodding along in traditional parenting groups while other mothers shared their perfectly organized systems and color-coded schedules, she wasn't sure she could handle another round of well-meaning but impossible-to-implement advice. Her hands trembled slightly as she checked her phone; ten minutes late already, typical of her ADHD timing.[1]

Taking a deep breath, she finally pushed open the car door and walked into the café. The sound of laughter drew her attention to a corner where a group of women sat surrounded by planners, coffee cups, and, was that a stack of unfolded laundry someone had brought along? "I found three days' worth of clean clothes in my dryer this morning," one mom was saying, "and honestly, I'm counting it as a win that they made it to the dryer at all!"

In that moment, Eleanor felt her shoulders relax for the first time in months. These weren't the Pinterest-perfect moms she'd encountered in other groups. These were her people.[3]

Finding your tribe as an ADHD parent isn't just about making friends; it's about connecting with others who truly understand the unique challenges of navigating parenthood with a neurodivergent brain. It's about finding people who won't judge you for showing up with mismatched socks or forgetting the bake sale for the third time this year.[1, 2]

Beatrice, a regular at the support group, often shares how she found her tribe through a combination of in-person and online connections. "I started with a Facebook group for ADHD moms," she explains. "Just reading other mothers' posts helped me feel less alone. When I discovered that three other moms in the group lived nearby, we created our own weekly coffee meetup. Now we're each other's emergency contacts for school pickup and share calendar reminders for important dates."

Building your support network doesn't have to be overwhelming. Start where you feel most comfortable, whether that's joining an online community, reaching out to other parents at your child's school, or connecting with local ADHD support organizations.[1] The key is finding people who understand that sometimes the biggest victory of your day might be remembering to sign that permission slip on the first try.

Jessica found her tribe in an unexpected place: the waiting room of her daughter's occupational therapy office. "I was frantically trying to reschedule an appointment I'd forgotten about when another mom overheard and said, 'Oh, you must have ADHD too!' We ended up starting a text group with other parents from the clinic. Now we help each other remember appointments and share strategies for managing medication schedules and school communications."[3]

Your support system might also include professional connections who understand ADHD parenting challenges. A therapist who specializes in ADHD, an understanding pediatrician, or teachers who 'get it' can become valuable members of your tribe. These professionals can offer guidance while respecting the unique ways ADHD affects your parenting journey.[1, 2]

Remember that building your tribe takes time, and it's okay to start small. Maybe it begins with one understanding friend who doesn't mind when you text at midnight because you've just remembered it's your turn to bring snacks to tomorrow's soccer game. Or perhaps it's finding an online community where you can share your struggles and victories with others who truly understand.[3]

As Adriana, a mother of three, often reminds newcomers to our support group, "We're not looking for perfect parents here; we're looking for real ones. The kind who understand why you might have three different calendar apps on your phone and still forget dentist appointments. The kind who celebrate with you when you remember to pack lunch before leaving the house, because they know what a victory that can be."[3]

Your tribe is out there, waiting to welcome you with understanding nods, practical solutions, and perhaps most importantly, the reassurance that you're not alone in this journey of ADHD parenthood.[1, 2, 3]

Communication Strategies: Explaining ADHD Needs to Family and Friends

Carly stood in her kitchen, tears welling up as her mother-in-law rearranged the carefully organized chaos of her cupboards for the third time this month. "I'm just trying to help," Belinda insisted, not understanding that her well-intentioned organizing was actually making things harder for Carly's ADHD brain. This scene plays out in countless homes, where well-meaning family and friends struggle to understand the unique needs of someone with ADHD.[2, 4]

Explaining ADHD to loved ones often feels like trying to describe colors to someone who's never seen them. It's frustrating, emotionally draining, and sometimes feels impossible. But as I've learned through both personal experience and helping other ADHD moms, effective communication about our needs isn't just possible; it's essential for our well-being and family harmony.[2, 4]

Let me share how Natasha, one of the moms in my support group, transformed her family dynamics through thoughtful communication. "I used to get so angry when my husband would say things like 'just try harder' or 'you need to focus more,'" she explains. "Then I realized he wasn't being dismissive; he genuinely didn't understand how my brain works." Jessica started by sharing simple analogies that helped her family grasp her experience.[4, 5] "I explained that my ADHD brain is like having 50 browser tabs open at once, all playing different videos at full volume. That image clicked for them in a way medical explanations never did."

When communicating with family about ADHD needs, timing and approach make all the difference. Choose calm moments for important conversations, not times of stress or conflict.[4] Start with appreciation for their desire to help, then explain specifically how their support would be most effective. For instance, instead of saying "Stop reorganizing my things," Rachel eventually told her mother-in-law, "I really appreciate your desire to help me stay organized. My brain needs visual cues to function well, which is why I keep frequently used items in open containers. Would you like to help me label these containers to make my system clearer?"[3]

Val, another mom from our group, developed what she calls her "ADHD translation guide" for family members. "Sometimes I get overwhelmed and can't articulate what I need in the moment," she shares. "So I created a simple guide that explains common situations. When I say 'I'm spinning,' my family knows I need quiet time to regroup. When I say 'my tabs are full,' they know to help me write things down rather than giving me more verbal instructions."[4]

For friends and extended family, the conversation might need a different approach. Vanessa found success in being direct but positive: "I tell them, 'My brain works a bit differently, and while it gives me some amazing creative abilities, it also means I need certain accommodations to function at my best.'"[2, 5] She follows this with specific examples of how they can help, like sending text reminders for plans or understanding when she needs to limit social commitments.

Children, especially older ones, can also benefit from understanding their parents' ADHD needs.[5] Wendy involves her teenagers in creating family systems that work for everyone. "We have weekly 'brain storming' sessions where we talk openly about our challenges and brainstorm solutions together," she explains. "It's helped them understand why I sometimes need quiet time to complete tasks, and they've even started adopting some of my coping strategies for their own use."

Remember that helping others understand your ADHD isn't a one-time conversation; it's an ongoing dialogue.[4, 5] Be patient with yourself and others as you develop these communication skills. Not everyone will fully understand your experience, and that's okay. Focus on those who make the effort to learn and support you.

Perhaps most importantly, approach these conversations with self-compassion.[2] Your needs aren't burdensome or unreasonable; they're valid requirements for your brain to function at its best. By clearly communicating these needs to family and friends, you're not just helping yourself; you're also modeling important self-advocacy skills for your children and contributing to greater understanding of neurodiversity in your community.[4, 5]

Building Reciprocal Support Systems: Give and Take in ADHD Relationships

Astrid stared at her phone, tears welling up as she read another message from a friend she'd let down. She'd forgotten to pick up school supplies for their kids' joint project, again. The guilt was overwhelming, not just about this incident, but about all the times her ADHD had affected her relationships. She felt like she was always taking support but never giving enough back.[6]

This feeling of imbalance in relationships is common among ADHD moms. We often worry we're the ones always needing help, constantly apologizing for forgotten commitments or last-minute cancellations.[6] But building strong, reciprocal support systems isn't about keeping a perfect score; it's about finding ways to give and receive support that work with our unique brain wiring.[6]

Take Carmen, who struggled with traditional playdate hosting but discovered she could contribute to her mom group in different ways. "I'm terrible at organizing structured activities," she shares, "but I'm great at spontaneous adventures. Now, when other moms need a break, I'm the one who takes all the kids to explore the local creek or create massive art projects. It's chaotic and fun, and the kids love it."[6]

The key to building reciprocal relationships is recognizing and leveraging your strengths. Maybe you're not the mom who remembers every birthday, but you might be the one who can drop everything to help during an emergency. Perhaps you struggle with consistent check-ins but excel at providing emotional support during late-night anxiety calls.[6]

Caroline found her balance through what she calls her "support swap" system. "I partner with another mom who's super-organized but struggles with creative projects," she explains. "She helps me remember school deadlines and appointment times, while I help her brainstorm solutions for her kids' challenges and plan engaging family activities. We both contribute what comes naturally to us."[6]

Building reciprocal support systems also means being honest about your limitations. Esther learned this lesson after repeatedly overcommitting to volunteer work. "Now I'm upfront about my ADHD," she says. "I tell people I might not be reliable for regular commitments, but I'm great at one-time projects where I can hyperfocus and get things done quickly."[2]

The magic happens when we stop trying to reciprocate in conventional ways and start embracing our unique abilities to give back. Gabriela, a mom of three, discovered this when she felt guilty about always needing schedule reminders from other parents. "Instead of beating myself up about it, I started offering what I could; my creativity in crisis-solving, my willingness to laugh at the chaos, and my genuine enthusiasm for celebrating other moms' victories, no matter how small."[6]

Here's what I've learned about creating sustainable reciprocal relationships:

Start with honesty. Let people know about your ADHD and how it affects your ability to give and receive support. This transparency often leads to more understanding and flexible arrangements.[2]

Look for complementary partnerships. Find friends whose strengths complement your weaknesses and vice versa. These relationships often become the most naturally reciprocal.[6]

Offer what comes easily to you. If you're great at brainstorming solutions, be the friend who helps problem-solve. If you're good in a crisis, be the emergency contact. Play to your strengths rather than forcing yourself into traditional support roles.[6]

Accept help graciously. Remember that allowing others to support you is itself a gift; it helps them feel valued and needed. As Faye, one of my coaching clients, realized, "When I stopped apologizing for needing help and started openly appreciating it, my friendships actually grew stronger."[2]

Most importantly, remember that reciprocity doesn't have to be immediate or even. Some seasons you might need more support, while in others you'll be the one giving more. The goal isn't perfect balance but creating sustainable relationships where everyone feels valued and supported in ways that work for them.[6]

Helen stared at her laptop screen, her heart racing as notifications flooded in: three urgent work emails, a text about her daughter's forgotten lunch box, and a calendar reminder for a meeting she hadn't prepared for. In that moment, she embodied the daily reality of every working ADHD mom trying to juggle career and family responsibilities.

As we've explored throughout this book, success in balancing work and family life with ADHD isn't about achieving perfection; it's about creating sustainable systems that work with our unique brain wiring. We've seen how mothers can transform their tendency to hyperfocus into a professional asset, using time-blocking techniques that accommodate both work projects and family commitments. Caroline's story showed us how being open about her ADHD needs led to workplace accommodations that benefited her entire team.

The journey of a working ADHD mom often feels like conducting an orchestra where every instrument plays at a different tempo. Yet, as we've discovered, our ADHD traits can become our greatest strengths in the workplace when we learn to harness them effectively. Our ability to think creatively, handle multiple streams of information, and find innovative solutions to problems are invaluable skills in today's dynamic work environment.

Remember the technique of creating visual project management systems? This approach not only can improve work performance but also provides a model for children about adapting environments to work with, rather than against, their needs. These moments of challenge-turned-triumph remind us that our ADHD isn't a barrier to professional success; it's often the catalyst for innovative solutions that benefit everyone.

As you move forward in your career journey, remember that advocating for your needs isn't a sign of weakness; it's a demonstration of professional self-awareness. Whether it's requesting flexible work hours to accommodate medication schedules, setting up a more visual workspace, or establishing clear communication protocols with your team, these adaptations help you bring your best self to both your work and family life.

The strategies we've explored, from creating ADHD-friendly workspaces to developing effective communication systems, are tools in your professional toolkit, ready to be adapted and personalized for your specific situation. Opening up to people about her ADHD can help us to see that understanding and support often come when we're brave enough to ask for what we need.

As you continue navigating the dual challenges of career and motherhood with ADHD, remember that you're not just managing; you're pioneering new ways of working that could benefit future generations of neurodivergent professionals. Your journey matters, and your success, however you define it, is worth celebrating. This chapter has shown the benefits of building a village, finding your tribe and connecting with like-minded individuals, having clear communication strategies to explain your AHD to others, and supporting people using your skills.

For now, take a moment to appreciate how far you've come in understanding and working with your ADHD brain in the professional world and family life. You're not just surviving as a working ADHD mom; you're showing your children, colleagues, and the world that different doesn't mean deficient. Your unique approach to balancing work and family life might be exactly what your workplace and family need, even if they don't know it yet. You'll be a real asset to other people and can support them, using your unique skills.

Conclusion

As we close this transformative journey together, let's celebrate a profound truth we've discovered: your ADHD isn't a limitation; it's a unique lens through which you experience and enhance the world of motherhood. Throughout these pages, we've explored how to transform what society often sees as challenges into your distinct advantages, turning scattered thoughts into creative solutions and impulsive energy into spontaneous joy with your children.

Think back to where you started this book. Perhaps you were feeling overwhelmed, questioning your ability to juggle the countless balls of motherhood while managing your ADHD. Now you're equipped with practical strategies that work with your brain rather than against it. From your kitchen table command center to your personalized digital systems, you've learned how to create structures that support rather than constrain you. You understand how to harness hyperfocus as a superpower, build routines that actually stick, and cultivate support systems that truly get you.

But the most powerful transformation isn't in the systems you've built; it's in the way you now see yourself. Your out-of-the-box thinking isn't a flaw; it's the secret ingredient that helps you solve parenting challenges creatively. Your intense emotions aren't a weakness; they're what make you deeply attuned to your children's needs. Even your struggles serve a greater purpose, teaching your children invaluable lessons about resilience, adaptation, and self-acceptance.

Remember, this journey isn't about achieving perfection; it's about progress and self-discovery. There will be days when systems fall apart, when the mental load feels crushing, or when you find yourself slipping into old patterns. That's not failure; that's being human. What matters is your willingness to begin again, to adjust your approach, and to keep moving forward with self-compassion.

Your ADHD motherhood journey is uniquely yours, and it's still unfolding. Take these strategies and make them your own. Modify them to fit your life, your family, and your beautiful ADHD brain. Share your discoveries with other mothers, because every time you open up about your experiences, you help build a more understanding and supportive community for all of us.

You're not just surviving motherhood with ADHD; you're revolutionizing it. Every time you embrace your unique approach to parenting, you help create a world that better understands and celebrates neurodiversity. Your children are watching and learning from your example, seeing what it means to live authentically and turn challenges into strengths.

So what's your next step? Start small, but start today. Choose one strategy from this book that resonated most strongly with you. Perhaps it's setting up your command center, establishing a simple morning routine, or reaching out to build your support network. Take that first step, knowing that it doesn't have to be perfect; it just has to be a beginning.

You have everything you need to thrive as an ADHD mom. Your unique brain wiring isn't an obstacle to overcome; it's the key to becoming the mother you're meant to be. Trust yourself, embrace your journey, and remember that you're part of a powerful community of ADHD moms who are rewriting the rules of motherhood, one beautiful, chaotic, creative day at a time.

Now, close this book and take that first step. Your ADHD motherhood adventure is waiting, and you're ready to embrace it with all the courage, creativity, and authenticity that make you uniquely you. You've got this, mama, and your best chapter is just beginning.

Bibliography

Barkley, R. A. (2015). Attention-Deficit Hyperactivity Disorder: A Handbook for Diagnosis and Treatment (4th ed.). The Guilford Press.

Brown, T. E. (2013). A New Understanding of ADHD in Children and Adults: Executive Function Impairments. Routledge.

Dodson, W. (2021). ADHD 2.0: New Science and Essential Strategies for Thriving with Distraction. Ballantine Books.

Hollowell, E. M., & Ratey, J. J. (2011). Driven to Distraction: Recognizing and Coping with Attention Deficit Disorder from Childhood Through Adulthood. Anchor Books.

Kohlberg, J., & Nadeau, K. (2016). ADD-Friendly Ways to Organize Your Life: Strategies that Work from an Acclaimed Professional Organizer and a Renowned ADD Clinician. Routledge.

Matlen, T. (2014). The Queen of Distraction: How Women with ADHD Can Conquer Chaos, Find Focus, and Get More Done. New Harbinger Publications.

Nadeau, K. G. (2015). The ADHD Guide to Career Success: Harness your Strengths, Manage your Challenges. Routledge.

Nadeau, K. G., Littman, E. B., & Quinn, P. O. (2015). Understanding Girls with ADHD: How They Feel and Why They Do What They Do. Advantage Books.

Pera, G. (2008). Is It You, Me, or Adult A.D.D.? Stopping the Roller Coaster When Someone You Love Has Attention Deficit Disorder. 1201 Alarm Press.

Quinn, P. O., & Nadeau, K. G. (2012). Understanding Women with AD/HD. Advantage Books.

Ratey, N. A. (2008). The Disorganized Mind: Coaching Your ADHD Brain to Take Control of Your Time, Tasks, and Talents. St. Martin's Griffin.

Solden, S. (2012). Women with Attention Deficit Disorder: Embrace Your Differences and Transform Your Life. Understanding ADHD.

Thank You for Reading!

I hope you found *Thriving as an ADHD Mom: Proven Systems to Organize Life, Balance Work & Family* helpful and enjoyable!
Your feedback is invaluable to me and helps others discover this book.

If you could take a moment to **leave a review**, I'd greatly appreciate it. Scan the QR code below to leave your review:

Visit the Cantelune Press website for more compassionate books that meet you where you are!

https://cantelunepress.com/

Thank you,

Patty R. Adams

www.ingramcontent.com/pod-product-compliance
Lightning Source LLC
Chambersburg PA
CBHW071517120626
46550CB00006B/2254